W9-ACV-310

REAL JUSTICE

JAILED FOR LIFE FOR BEING BLACK

• • •

THE STORY OF RUBIN "HURRICANE" CARTER

BILL SWAN

WITH A FOREWORD BY
KEN KLONSKY

LORIMER

JAMES LORIMER & COMPANY LTD., PUBLISHERS
TORONTO

James Lorimer & Company Ltd., Publishers acknowledges the support of the Ontario Arts Council. We acknowledge the financial support of the Government of Canada through the Canada Book Fund for our publishing activities. We acknowledge the support of the Canada Council for the Arts which last year invested $24.3 million in writing and publishing throughout Canada. We acknowledge the Government of Ontario through the Ontario Media Development Corporation's Ontario Book Initiative.

Canada Council for the Arts
ONTARIO ARTS COUNCIL
CONSEIL DES ARTS DE L'ONTARIO

Cover image: The Canadian Press/AP

Library and Archives Canada Cataloguing in Publication

Swan, Bill, 1939-, author
    Real justice : jailed for life for being black : the story of Rubin "Hurricane" Carter / Bill Swan ; with an introduction by Ken Klonsky.

(Real justice)
Includes bibliographical references and index.
Issued in print and electronic formats.
ISBN 978-1-4594-0665-0 (pbk.).--ISBN 978-1-4594-0666-7 (bound).--ISBN 978-1-4594-0667-4 (epub)

    1. Carter, Rubin, 1937-2014--Juvenile literature. 2. Prisoners--United States--Biography--Juvenile literature. 3. Boxers (Sports)--United States--Biography--Juvenile literature. 4. Racism--United States--Juvenile literature. 5. Judicial error--United States--Juvenile literature. 6. Criminal justice, Administration of--United States--Juvenile literature. I. Title. II. Title: Hurricane Carter : the story of Rubin "Hurricane" Carter. III. Series: Real justice (Toronto, Ont.)

HV6248.C34S92 2014   j365'.6092   C2014-903028-2
                                                C2014-903029-0

James Lorimer & Company Ltd.,
Publishers
317 Adelaide Street West, Suite 1002
Toronto, ON, Canada
M5V 1P9
www.lorimer.ca

Distributed in the United States by:
Orca Book Publishers
P.O. Box 468
Custer, WA, USA
98240-0468

Printed and bound in Canada
Manufactured by Friesens Corporation in Altona, Manitoba, Canada in August 2014.
Job #205782

TO RUBIN CARTER AND JOHN ARTIS

CONTENTS

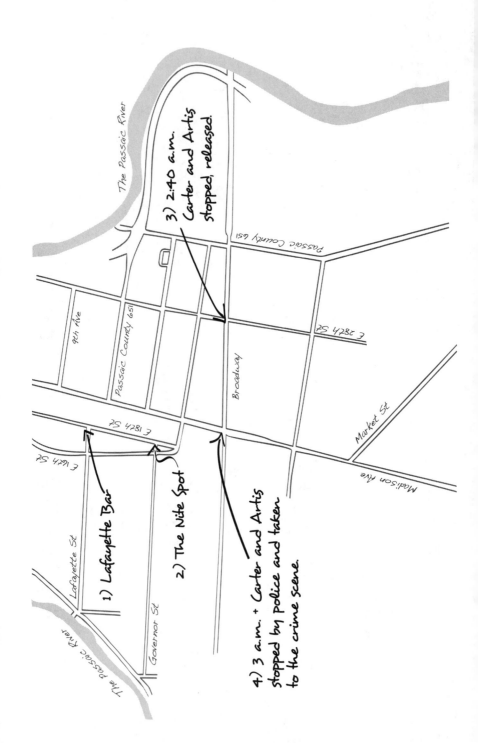

The Passaic River

3) 2:40 a.m.
Carter and Artis
stopped, released.

Passaic County 651

9th Ave

Passaic County 651

E 28th St

Broadway

E 18th St

Market St

E 16th St

Lafayette St

Madison Ave

1) Lafayette Bar

Governor St

2) The Nite Spot

The Passaic River

4) 3 a.m. + Carter and Artis
stopped by police and taken
to the crime scene.

FOREWORD

A truly free man can never really lose his liberty, because liberty is a quality that comes from within. Back in 1966, Rubin "Hurricane" Carter, a feared middleweight boxer, was convicted and imprisoned for a crime he did not commit — a triple murder at a bar in Paterson, New Jersey. He narrowly escaped the electric chair. This man, with no more than a Grade 8 education, then wrote a book from prison, *The Sixteenth Round: From Number 1 Contender to Number 45472,* that inspired people such as Muhammad Ali and Bob Dylan to join his cause, helping to overturn his first conviction.

In 1974, Rubin was convicted again of the same crime, but he continued to maintain his innocence by refusing to wear the clothes, eat the food, or do any work to help the prison function. He was forced to endure years in solitary confinement in a hole below the ground, but he would never give in to the attempt to make him behave as if he were a criminal. Yet he was as angry "as a black bear in mating season who wasn't getting his own." This anger at the system and "everything that moved" was about to destroy Rubin, until one day he looked into a mirror on the way to the prison hospital:

"I saw a monster. Bulging out of its head were two big, glassy eyes. The skin was stretched so tightly over its face that it was shining. Its lips were thin and drawn back, revealing big yellow teeth, rotted gums, and a perpetual grimace of pure sadistic delight. Hatred and bitterness had taken me over."

He knew then that if he was going to escape the mentality of the prison, the mentality of violence that would have caused his death, he would have to change. He would have to educate himself; he would have to understand the forces in the world that had shaped him; and he would have to rise above the place where he now found himself. He went on to spend ten years reading what the best and brightest minds in the world had written. He studied world religions to understand the spiritual forces in the world that most of us pay no attention to. He learned internal discipline. In his second and final book, *Eye of the Hurricane: My Path from Darkness to Freedom*, he tells the reader:

"To deal with the constant hunger, I had to control my many cravings, which meant controlling both body and mind. I had to overcome all of those things that advertise your hunger: the growling of your stomach or a headache or visions of your favorite foods. Hunger and pain can be controlled by the mind. The physical body knows nothing about pain, heat, cold, time, or hunger, but the mind does. The mind then imposes its conditions upon the body, while our capacity to endure is far greater than we realize. Of course my career as a professional boxer, having the stamina and endurance to go the distance many times, came in handy in this regard."

This internal discipline allowed him to emerge from prison a better person, an influential, respected, even a much-loved person.

Whenever Rubin Carter spoke to high-school audiences (and that is where I met him for the first time), he had two related messages: "Dare to dream!" and "Go the distance!" Dreaming is necessary to find out what you want to do, but dreaming is the easy part. Going the distance, like a boxer in a championship fight, is the hard part. Most people cannot go the distance. They find many excuses to quit. The most common excuse is that the goal might take too much time to achieve. Trying to free an innocent person from prison can take more than a decade. When Rubin was freed from prison by Judge H. Lee Sarokin, he came to Toronto, Canada, joined with like-minded people, helping to free more than twenty wrongly convicted prisoners, both in Canada and the United States.

The quality of perseverance, of going the distance, was never on better display than during his fight with advanced cancer. In October of 2011, I was present when he was given three months to live. I write this Foreword in March 2014, as Rubin clings to life by a slender thread. Rubin Carter was never knocked out in the boxing ring, and he brought that determination to the end of his life. Despite the extreme pain he faced, he had the heart of a champion; you knew he would never go down easily.

In his last days, he wrote a plea to the office of Ken Thompson, the Brooklyn District Attorney, to ask that the wrongly convicted David McCallum be given a hearing:

"Wonderful things have been given to me in my life, my freedom from a place of living hell granted by the brave Judge H. Lee Sarokin, awards I've received from every corner of the globe, and dedicated people who worked for no payment beyond the thanks I was able to give. David McCallum was incarcerated two weeks before my release. I was then reborn into the miracle of this wonderful world from which Death is now waiting to claim me. I'm looking Death straight in the eye; he's got me on the ropes, but I won't back down. Now I ask Ken Thompson to look straight in the eye of truth, a tougher customer than death, and not back down either. Just as my own verdict 'was predicated on racism rather than reason and on concealment rather than disclosure,' so too was Mr. McCallum's. My aim in helping this fine man is to give him the help that I received as a wrongly convicted man."

Even in death he remembered others like him who are suffering needlessly every single day. He was daring to dream that David McCallum would be freed. He was going the distance for as long as he could still breathe.

— Ken Klonsky

CHAPTER ONE

THE SHOOTING

Four people were in the Lafayette Bar and Grill in Paterson, New Jersey, in the early morning of June 17, 1966.

Behind the bar was bartender Jimmy Oliver, doing what bartenders do: tending bar. Oliver lived in a third-floor apartment above the bar. The bar was in what then was known in Paterson as a white area. Though the law was changing, segregation of races in the U.S. was very real, Some said Oliver would not serve blacks.

A customer, Fred Nauyoks, sixty years old and a regular at the Lafayette, occupied his favourite bar stool. Two stools down, where he had been for most of the evening, sat Willie Marins, a forty-three-year-old machinist.

Partially hidden behind a side door was Hazel Tanis, a fifty-one-year-old waitress. She had arrived shortly before, following her shift at the Westmount Country

Club. She greeted the three others in the bar, and then went to the washroom.

At about 2:20 a.m., two black men walked into the bar. Both were tall and thin. One had a pencil-thin moustache.

One carried a shotgun, the other a handgun.

Without hesitation, the bartender wheeled quickly away from the cash register. In one motion, he hurled an empty bottle at the man with the shotgun. The bottle smashed against the wall. Before it did, the bartender turned to run.

The shotgun came up to hip height. One blast caught Oliver in his first step. From less than two metres away, the blast ripped a hole in the bartender's back. He fell dead, two bottles of liquor at his feet.

Almost at the same time, the man with the handgun took aim and fired. The bullet hit Nauyoks below the right earlobe, into the base of the brain. He died instantly, his shot glass still full, the change for the drink still on the bar.

Still holding the handgun, the second assailant then turned and aimed at Marins. He fired again. This bullet caught Marins near the left temple and exited from his forehead, just above the left eye.

The man with the shotgun took one or two steps farther into the bar. That's when he saw Hazel Tanis.

"Oh, no!" she cried, and cowered on the floor.

The man with the shotgun stepped around the pool table and looked at Tanis. From the hip, he levelled the shotgun and fired. The blast caught the waitress in the upper right arm and right breast.

The second man held the handgun at arm's length and fired five times: *bang, bang, bang, bang, bang*, catching Tanis in the right breast, lower abdomen, and twice in the area of the hip and crotch. One shot missed.

The gunmen took a quick look around the room, then left through the same door they had entered. Outside, they walked around the corner to a white late-model car. They got in, and the car sped away.

Watching from the shadows of a nearby alley, Alfred Bello breathed a sigh of relief.

From a window above the bar, Patricia Graham had watched the two men enter the car. She noted the dark licence plate that was not from New Jersey. The car braked briefly, revealing distinctive brake lights shaped like a butterfly, before it was out of sight.

★   ★   ★

For Alfred Bello, it had been a difficult night. The goal had been simple: He and Arthur Dexter Bradley had planned to break into a small warehouse.

Bello's job was to be lookout. He was to hide himself in the shadows and watch for police, or passersby, or anyone who might stumble along.

Traffic was sparse. It was not a high-traffic area. It was after two in the morning. The warehouse was in a light industrial area of Paterson, New Jersey. The Lafayette Bar and Grill was right around the corner.

One white car drove by. Bello waited.

A few minutes later, the same car came down the street. The first to admit he was no genius, Bello took note. The car had circled the block. His Spidey sense gripped him: *plainclothes cops?*

While his buddy waited with a tire iron — the only break-and-entry tool they had — Bello longed for a cigarette. He left his lookout post and walked down the street toward the Lafayette Bar.

Approaching the bar, he saw the same white car parked half out on the street. Then came noises that, at first, he took for drums. But the Lafayette had no band, played no music. *Oh-oh. Poof, bang, bang, bang.* Bello stopped. Something was up.

Around the corner from the front entrance of the bar, two black men walked toward him, laughing and chatting. At first he thought they were detectives. One carried a shotgun or rifle; the other held a handgun.

But three car lengths away, Bello saw his mistake. The noise he heard was not drums. These guys meant business. He spun on his heel and ran. Bello was not a fast runner at any time, and his high-heeled boots slowed him even more. At the first chance, he ducked into a laneway, flattened himself against the fence, and waited.

He heard the car doors slam. He peeked out.

The white car peeled away. As it passed the alley, the car brake lights came on, lighting up the back of the car. The car hesitated before speeding away, headed for 16th Avenue. A block away, the car turned left and was gone.

Bello knew — who said he was not a genius? — that something had gone down.

He came out of the alley and continued down Lafayette to the corner of 18th Avenue. He entered the bar through the front door.

From the doorway, he found it hard to see in the dimly lit bar. When his eyes adjusted, he could make out one man wandering blindly around the room. The man stumbled. He held one hand against the massive wound in his head. With the other, he held on to a pole by the pool table.

At the bar, one man rested as though he had had one drink too many. A cigarette smouldered between his fingers. His other hand still gripped a fresh drink. Pocket change lay on the bar. The man had a bullet hole in his head.

Farther down the bar, he could hear someone, a woman, moaning in pain and shock.

A second woman entered the bar from a side door. Holding the front of a raincoat closed in front of her, she hesitated.

"Don't come in," Bello said to the young woman. *Pat, wasn't it? Pat Graham?* He had seen her before.

He came around the bar and now could see the wounded woman lying on her side. Blood soaked her clothes. Bello knelt for a moment, lifted the woman's head, and then turned back to the bar.

The woman in the raincoat ignored him. She entered, and screamed. She knelt by the wounded woman.

"I'll get help," Pat said to the woman. She turned and left through the side door.

Bello hesitated.

He should call the police. *And tell them what? I was waiting to do a break and enter, and discovered . . .*

For an instant, his better instincts took hold.

Call police. He had to. The other woman, Pat, had seen him.

A dime. He'd need a dime to call police. Behind the bar, the cash register was open.

That's when he saw the body of the bartender. He was face down on the floor. A shotgun or something had blasted a hole in his back.

Bello stepped over the body and reached into the open drawer. He fished out a dime with one finger. He hesitated.

Why not?

Quickly, he grabbed at the bills in the drawer. One handful. Two handfuls. Tens. Fives. Some bills fell on the floor. *Don't drop the dime.*

At the pay phone, he dialled zero for the operator, asked for the police. "A shooting," he said. "The Lafayette."

He left the bar and headed up the street. There he met his break-in buddy, Bradley, and gave him a quick version of what had taken place.

Bradley looked at the fistful of bills in Bello's hand.

"Yeah," Bello said, showing handfuls of fives and tens, into Bradley's hand. "Give me my half later."

"Let's get out of here," Bradley said.

Bello shook his head.

"I gotta go back," Bello said. "The woman who lives upstairs saw me. She knows me."

Maybe the dude with the head wound, too, he thought. *And the wounded woman, although she didn't look like she was long for this earth.* He had to go back.

Three squad cars arrived almost all at once, sirens wailing, bubble gum lights on top, flashing round and round.

Bello sprinted back to the bar. He slowed to a walk as he saw Pat Graham again at the side door, talking to a police officer.

2

CHAPTER TWO

NIGHT ON THE TOWN

Rubin "Hurricane" Carter liked to party, of that there was no doubt. If he could combine business with the partying, so much the better.

This was exactly what he was doing the night of June 16 and in the early morning of June 17, 1966.

Rubin was a professional boxer. Not just any pro boxer. Two years before, he had a shot at the middle-weight championship of the world.

Of the world: That is worth repeating. In Paterson, New Jersey, he was a local hero, particularly in the black community.

The early part of that evening he spent at home with his wife and young daughter, watching television. The domestic bliss ended with a call from his new business advisor, Nate Sermond. Talks had been going on about a fight in South America. Could Hurricane meet him at his club to clear up some business?

In the first ten weeks of 1966, Hurricane had five fights: two wins, two losses, and a draw. But he hadn't fought since March 8. A layoff of more than three months. Not one to train hard with no fight on his calendar, Hurricane was beginning to feel soft, itched for a return to the ring. His lifestyle didn't help, either, and had to have affected his bank account.

It was almost midnight when he left home. His Cadillac was blocked in his driveway, so he drove his leased business car, a white 1966 Dodge Polara. A few blocks away, he picked up the friendly neighbourhood drunk, John "Bucks" Royster. Hurricane had grown up in Paterson. He still lived there. He had vowed never to forget his origins and the people, especially the black people, of his hometown.

In the 1960s, Paterson, New Jersey, only forty kilometres (about twenty-five miles) from New York City, had a population of about 120,000. A third were black. The town was firmly divided. Blacks were treated poorly.

As Hurricane pulled up at Club La Petite, a young man with a wide grin poked his head in the open passenger window.

"Hey, Rube, how's it going?" Nineteen-year-old John Artis had been drinking, but that just made him friendlier. Artis always had a happy grin. He was two years out of high school, where he had been a track star. He planned to go to college.

Hurricane gave him a dismissive wave.

"How 'bout a ride to the Nite Spot?" Artis asked.

"Maybe later," Hurricane replied. "Got some business to do."

In the bar, Hurricane's manager had disappointing news. The promoters of a possible fight in South America would cover the cost of only two plane tickets: for Hurricane and his manager. He couldn't take his own sparring partner.

"I can't take the chance on hiring some chump down there," Hurricane said. "Tell 'em it's no deal."

"It could be a deal breaker," his manager replied.

"Better break the deal than my head," Hurricane replied. He knew all too well the need for a sparring partner. Conditioning was fine: the road work, the body bag, the punching bag. But a boxer hones skills in practice, sparring with other boxers.

"You need this fight," his manager warned.

"They don't know that," Hurricane said. "Push 'em."

Outside, Artis waited by Hurricane's car like a puppy dog near its master.

Hurricane dropped Artis at the Nite Spot, a nearby

club, and then drove himself to Ritchie's Hideaway to hear a favoured band.

By 2:00 a.m., Hurricane ended up back at the Nite Spot. A friend, Cathy McGuire, asked for a ride home for her and her mother. McGuire lived in a rough section of town. Hurricane agreed, and the trip took about ten minutes. He returned to the Nite Spot.

About that time, Eddie Rawls returned to the Nite Spot from the hospital.

"Sorry about your dad," Hurricane said.

Eddie Rawls was the bartender at the Nite Spot. Earlier that evening, in a bar in another part of the city, Rawls's stepfather had been killed by a shotgun blast. Rawls had been called to the hospital and was just now returning.

Rawls mumbled his thanks.

Shortly after, Hurricane realized that he was short of cash. This was in the days before ATM machines; if you wanted cash, you had to get it from the bank during office hours. Luckily, Hurricane kept cash at home. Since the evening was not over, he thought it worth a trip home to get more.

But despite his happy marriage to Mae Thelma, Hurricane knew that she might kick up a fuss at this late hour. He needed some company — male company — if he were to return home.

Outside the bar, "Bucks" Royster was propped against a cigarette machine. Hurricane asked if he wanted to go for a ride.

John Artis stepped forward. "Can I come?" he asked.

It was a request that changed Artis's life forever.

For the eager young man — barely out of high school — it was a thrill to be near this local hero.

Royster was in his usual condition — drunk — but Artis looked sober. Hurricane tossed the keys to Artis.

"You drive," he said.

Artis couldn't believe his ears. *Him? Driving The Hurricane's car? Would his buddies ever believe that?*

Perhaps if Hurricane had known that Artis had already drunk too much and had barfed in the alley, he would not have trusted the kid.

But the white Dodge Polara was only his training car, used for hauling equipment to and from his training camp. It wasn't as though he was letting the kid drive his Cadillac Eldorado — the luxury American car of the 1960s.

Artis got behind the wheel. Hurricane sprawled out in the back seat.

Less than three minutes from Hurricane's home, a police car pulled them over.

While one officer sauntered up to the driver's door, a

second officer stood behind, checking the plates.

"Ownership and driver's licence, sir," said the officer.

Artis lost some of his boyish grin. Being stopped by a cop is never pleasant; being stopped while black in Paterson, New Jersey, was definitely not pleasant.

Artis fumbled with his wallet and handed over his licence. He was obviously confused about the request for the ownership.

"It's on the steering post," Hurricane said, shifting to a sitting position.

The officer swung his flashlight into the back seat.

"Oh, it's you, Hurricane," he said. "How ya doing?" Hurricane and Sergeant Theodore Capter knew each other; this was Capter's regular patrol area.

Hurricane asked why they had been stopped. He had his suspicions: a young black man driving a late-model car. "Driving While Black." In New Jersey in 1966, police felt it their duty to stop a late-model car with a young black driver. Racism was blatant.

"We're just looking for a white car with two Negroes in it," the officer explained. He pointed with a finger as though doing difficult math: one, two, three. Artis, Royster, Hurricane.

"You're okay. On your way now."

The stop didn't surprise Hurricane. Police saw

Hurricane Carter as a troublemaker. He was "known to police" — he had a prison record. His high profile in the boxing world didn't change anything.

It was 2:40 a.m.

Hurricane and his companions continued to Hurricane's home. Hurricane added cash to his wallet. They returned to the Nite Spot.

By now it was nearly 3:00 a.m. on a Friday morning. Bars were closing. Running home to get cash had been the type of decision a guy makes when out drinking. Now he didn't need the cash.

He decided to call it a night.

First they dropped off Royster. A couple blocks later, Hurricane and Artis waited at a traffic light on Broadway for the light to change.

A police car pulled in front, cutting them off. An officer approached the car, gun drawn. But within sight of the driver's side, he began to holster his gun.

"Aw, it's you again, Hurricane. I'm sorry . . ."

It was Sergeant Capter again. But now another car arrived. (Police said later only two cars were involved; Hurricane claimed it was as many as five, with officers armed with pistols and shotguns.)

"Follow us," said the officer.

The parade of cars — three if you believe the police,

six if you believe Hurricane — made their way through the streets of Paterson, arriving shortly after 3:00 a.m. at the Lafayette Bar and Grill.

3

CHAPTER THREE

CRIME SCENE

The Lafayette, a small bar and grill on the corner of 18th Avenue and Lafayette Street, had attracted a small crowd. Several police cars, two ambulances, and the sound of their sirens had all disturbed the sleep of some area residents. Now the crowd stood around, shiftlessly, bathed in the light of the revolving red beacons, waiting for something to happen.

The crowd pulled back off the street as two or three more police cars arrived, a white Dodge sandwiched between them. The car pulled up to the side door of the bar.

"Outta the car," ordered one police officer.

The doors on each side of the white Dodge opened, and Hurricane and Artis got out. Never one to take orders in his stride, Hurricane scowled at the officer and hesitated briefly. A scowl from Hurricane was not something to be taken lightly. His scalp-bare haircut and Manchu moustache gave him the look of an ancient warrior.

A brief murmur ran through the three or four dozen people in the crowd. Hurricane. A world-ranked boxer in a city the size of Paterson drew attention. He had been on television, his pictures in the paper.

The crowd buzzed briefly with speculation.

But the cops said nothing, using their presence to keep the crowd across the narrow street.

Hurricane straightened the lapel of his jacket. From the number of cop cars, it was obvious that something serious had taken place. Now it dawned on him: *When they had been stopped the first time, Sergeant Capter said they had been looking for a car with two black men in it. That time there had been three of them.*

But after they had dropped off Royster, there were only two. Bingo.

Whatever had taken place here, he and Artis were being fingered for it. Something in the Lafayette Bar?

The Lafayette was only four blocks north of the Nite Spot, but they were worlds away. The Nite Spot attracted mostly black people. People said that the bartender at the Lafayette would not serve blacks.

In the crowd, Hurricane saw a young woman. She had been led out the side door of the grill, likely from the apartments above. Quietly, one officer brought her around to the rear of the car. A couple minutes later, the same cop led the woman back into the building.

Unknown to Hurricane, another person lurked in the crowd. Alfred Bello, who had stolen money from the cash register, kept near Patricia Graham. He tried to appear helpful to police. He eavesdropped while Patricia again described the car to police. He wanted to make sure his story matched.

Bello watched as one cop took the keys to Hurricane's car. Another ordered the boxer and Artis against the wall.

To Hurricane, the scene was chaotic. The crowd, largely white, pressed around his car. Police, armed with pistols and shotguns, kept the bystanders at bay. Years later Hurricane claimed one officer cocked the hammer on his pistol and pointed it at his head.

Eventually both he and Artis were pushed roughly into the back of a paddy wagon. The paddy wagon, used mostly for transporting drunks, stunk of puke and piss. Hurricane almost gagged.

Before they were seated, the vehicle lurched ahead, tossing them skidding around the metal wagon. It was in the days before seat belts, and in a paddy wagon, that wouldn't have mattered, anyway.

Hurricane had a lifetime of police harassment, some

of it deserved, much of it not. Now he worried about what this event was doing to his young companion. Artis was a good kid. He had been a track star in his high school. Now two years beyond graduation, his track coach was working to get him into college on a track scholarship. Involvement with police, even if he had done no wrong, wouldn't help.

At the hospital they were herded out of the paddy wagon. Under an armed escort, Hurricane and Artis were ushered into the emergency ward. Doctors and nurses hovered over and around a badly wounded man. His head was wrapped in bandages. Hurricane could see that a bullet had exited near the man's left eye. It was not a pretty sight.

"Can he talk?" one of the officers asked a doctor.

Reluctantly, the doctor consented. "But only for a moment."

A nurse helped raise the wounded man's head.

The man was weak and pale. Hurricane thought he was near death.

"Can you see clearly?" the officer asked the wounded man.

The man nodded.

"Are these the two men who shot you?"

Waiting for the answer took an eternity. With one

good eye, Willie Marins appeared to study the well-dressed boxer and his young companion. His gaze returned to Hurricane.

Finally, he rolled his head from side to side: no.

Hurricane almost cried with relief.

★   ★   ★

Police weren't through.

Before the night was over, Hurricane and Artis were subjected to hastily arranged lie detector tests. Both had voluntarily agreed to the tests.

The lie detector measures changes in blood pressure, pulse, and respiration rate. However, the results can't be used in court. Many factors can affect the results: anger, drinking, fear, even the need to go for a whiz.

The lie detector tests over, the two endured more questions. Hurricane offered to take a paraffin test. That would show if he had fired a gun that day. Paterson police didn't have a lab to make that test.

Artis, with little or no experience with police, assumed the whole thing was a big, giant mistake. *Mistakes get fixed, don't they?*

Hurricane, too, knew this was a mistake. But experience taught him that when police make mistakes, they don't like to admit it. He was also concerned about his young companion. Hurricane had seen Artis only a few times around the bars. He was a pleasant, polite kid. He didn't deserve this.

He had seen that police could push people and push people and push people until somehow they got the answers they wanted.

This time it did not work.

Late Friday afternoon, after thirteen hours in police custody, Hurricane and Artis walked out of the door of police headquarters. The local newspaper thought this worthy of a headline.

They released Hurricane's car, too. Hurricane was not really surprised when he opened the car door. The door liners and floor mats had been ripped out, the back seat tossed. Police had obviously been searching for anything that might link Hurricane and Artis to the crime.

He assumed they found nothing.

Life went on. The murder at the Lafayette Bar and Grill continued to baffle police. Usually, in a small city like Paterson, informants would come forward. The police would then have a name. They would know who to focus on, and would begin to build a case.

Nothing.

A reward of $10,500 was offered for information leading to a conviction.

Hurricane Carter travelled to South America. On August 6, 1966, he fought Rocky Rivero, losing a ten-round decision. He returned to his home in Paterson.

The summer passed. Then police picked up Alfred Bello for parole violation.

4

CHAPTER FOUR

HE'S MY BROTHER

Rubin Carter was five years old the day his older brother Jimmy came running into the apartment in tears.

"What's the matter?" he asked.

Through the tears and sobs, the story unfolded.

Jimmy had gone to the basement of the apartment building to fetch a pail of coal. In the 1940s, most homes were heated with coal. In houses, this meant the coal was stored in a bin in the basement.

In apartments, each family had its own storage bin.

When he arrived at the bin, Jimmy found another even older kid helping himself to the Carter family's coal.

He objected. He said it wasn't right. That coal belonged to the Carters, and . . .

The older kid didn't listen long. For his trouble, Jimmy received a beating that sent him scurrying upstairs, sobbing.

Jimmy was two years older than Rubin, but that didn't seem to matter. Rubin — his "Hurricane" name was added in his boxing career — knew this was not right. He ran downstairs and caught the same kid still scooping coal into a scuttle. Rubin put his head down and rushed headfirst into battle. Despite being outweighed by a boy three years older, he delivered a beating that sent the thief home, sobbing.

If he expected praise when his father got home, he was disappointed. His attempts to explain to his father fell on deaf ears.

The boy's mother complained to Rubin's father. Rubin tried to explain, but could not. Part of the blame may have been on Rubin's stumbling tongue: He stuttered badly. His father, an eloquent preacher, thought the stuttering came from nervous lying. He delivered the bare-buttocks beating he thought the Bible sanctioned. "Spare the rod and spoil the child." *Didn't the Good Book say that?* Rubin's father believed it did.

Rubin couldn't blame his troubled childhood on poverty. His parents did not neglect him. Many people tried to help him.

His father, a Baptist preacher, felt that the Bible said beatings were okay.

On at least one occasion, Rubin's father took him to police with a black eye and other bruises. Today this would be called abuse. In the 1940s spanking was normal, but what Rubin endured could only be called beatings.

Rubin was, at the very least, an "energetic" child. Today he undoubtedly would have been given a label: hyperactive, perhaps an attention disorder, and definitely a pronounced speech disorder.

In his first autobiography, Rubin blames much of his childhood frustrations on his speech. He could not clearly express his thoughts. When being disciplined at home or school — or with police — his stuttering became worse. His father, who as a child himself had stuttered, still thought stuttering meant lying.

If kids laughed at him when he tried to speak, his anger boiled over. His fists did not stutter. They delivered a very clear message. He had learned very early that he was stronger and tougher than others. While his tongue was awkward and stumbled and stuttered, his fists had no such problem. He learned to fight early.

He soon learned to enjoy fighting: a free-swinging battle in which he could allow his anger to race full throttle. High-spirited, he often put himself in trouble, perhaps confident he could fight his way out.

Once, he led the neighbourhood gang, the Apaches, past a storefront sale. On a lark, the group descended, grabbed clothes off the sidewalk racks, and raced away. At home, the loot didn't mean too much. He gave it away to his brothers and sisters. His father, seeing his children in new clothes that still bore the price tags, knew something was amiss.

Rubin got another beating, and this time his father called police. He was put on probation for two years.

But it was when he was fourteen that Rubin's childhood ended forever.

He and some gang members were visiting The Tubbs, a rather filthy swimming hole they saw as an escape from street life around them. After their swim, Rubin noticed a man watching from nearby bushes. The man approached and offered a watch, which one gang member took. But Rubin saw danger. As leader, he urged the others to run — and then found himself under attack.

In defence, Rubin smashed a glass soda pop bottle on the man's forehead. The man then grabbed him and tried to throw him over a cliff into the gully below. Rubin fought back. Grabbing the pocket knife he always carried — almost all boys and men at the time carried them — he stabbed the man in the leg. Rubin was thrown to the ground, and the man lay on top of him, as though in a sexual act.

Rubin still held his knife. He stabbed the man in the side over and over. Then he ran — only to return a few minutes later to retrieve his knife.

A day later, one gang member showed off a watch that he obviously could not afford. His parents were suspicious. Police were called. The man's name was inscribed on the back of the watch.

A businessman in his forties, the man was well-respected. Who would police believe — a businessman with a fine reputation or a black troublemaker who stuttered?

Rubin and three of his Apache gang friends were charged. The three friends were each sentenced to nine months in a home for boys. This included the kid who ended up with the watch.

But the judge saw Rubin as the leader, and his rough-and-tumble childhood caught up with him. The judge sentenced Rubin Carter to the Jamesburg State Home for Boys "until you are twenty-one years of age."

He was fourteen. His childhood was over.

★   ★   ★

Life at the Jamesburg State Home for Boys was supposed to help kids learn to grow up. Instead, it prepared them for life in prison.

The home resembled a military school. Inmates marched to work duty, marched to classes, marched to meals. Each inmate was assigned to one of the dozen or so cottages. This might seem like something out of *Harry Potter* — where the Sorting Hat assigns newcomers to a "house" in the school for magic.

At Jamesburg, the sorting was done largely by colour: blacks in cottages two, six, seven, and eight. Whites were assigned to cottages three, four, eleven, and twelve. Beyond that segregation, the boys were sorted again by age. This was a half-hearted attempt to protect younger inmates, some as young as eight, whose main crime was skipping school.

Sorting (or segregation) by colour now seems unthinkable. In the 1950s, it was not unusual. People of colour in the southern United States were discouraged from voting, and in many places, black people wouldn't be served at a lunch counter. Often, they had to ride in the back of the bus.

It was not only in the South.

In Paterson, New Jersey, Rubin Carter had grown up with discrimination. When he arrived in Jamesburg, what he saw was nothing new.

The first day, he reported to his assigned cottage. Instead of a welcome, he had managed to insult one of the "line sergeants" — an older inmate given responsibilities for others. Properly run, such a program could develop leaders. Poorly run, it was a licence to bully.

For the insult, "Chink," the line sergeant, invited Rubin to his "office." The office was the washroom and shower. Rubin was one of three or four others who had received similar invitations.

While he stood in line for his office time, Rubin could hear the beatings that Chink gave the others.

Chink was older. Bigger. Tougher.

When it came his turn, fourteen-year-old Rubin stammered, which was usual. He pretended to be scared, which he was not. Chink chuckled. But as Rubin squeezed by the larger youth to go into the "office," he turned on Chink.

In one motion, he swung his fist. Hard.

His uppercut caught Chink on the chin. The big kid crumpled, and as he fell, Rubin caught him twice more solidly on the jaw. He hit the floor, and lay unmoving.

When he came to, his supporters told him what happened. Chink vowed revenge.

Later that evening, Rubin and one other boy faced Chink and his army of half a dozen. Outnumbered, Rubin and the other kid, nicknamed "Little A," used baseball bats to defend themselves.

The two new allies, still armed with their trusty baseball bats, sent Chink and his friends packing. They also faced down four staff members, who came to restore order.

Jamesburg housed a variety of troubled children, including school truants, parole violators, sexual deviants, and one or two who had killed their own parents. Many were likely beyond redemption, waiting for the day they would be transferred to an adult prison.

In the eyes of the law, Rubin had been sentenced for a vicious stabbing of an upstanding citizen and the theft of an expensive watch. The law was blind to Rubin's claim that the man was a pedophile. That one of the other members of the Apaches had ended up with the watch didn't matter. The law didn't care that the pedophile would likely attack other children.

Experts thought Rubin was exactly where he belonged.

The pecking order went from older to younger. The older kids dominated simply because they were bigger and stronger. With Rubin, that didn't matter. He was big and strong for his age, and he didn't mind taking a punch or three. His fists decided his status.

Rubin had one firm rule: No one touched him.

One new staff member made that mistake. He ended up in the hospital with broken ribs and both arms in casts. Rubin ended up in solitary.

Superintendent Moore, the man in charge of Jamesburg, visited Rubin in his cell. He was a big man who overflowed any chair. His soft-spoken manner, backed up by his sheer size, had earned him Rubin's grudging respect. And he showed one quality that Rubin admired in any person: He was a straight shooter. He didn't bullshit, he didn't threaten.

"You hurt that man," he said, quietly.

Rubin bristled. "He had no business putting his hands on me! Next time he'll know!"

Superintendent Moore looked at Rubin. He talked carefully.

"There won't be a next time," he said. "You've hurt your last man at this institution."

Rubin did the translation. He would be transferred from Jamesburg to Annandale Reformatory, where they did everything but reform people.

"I . . . I . . . you . . . you," Rubin stuttered.

"Listen," said the superintendent. "I've got an offer for you."

Anything was better than Annandale. Rubin was ready to listen.

"Go three months without any trouble," Superintendent Moore said, "and I'll personally guarantee that you go home at the end of the ninety days."

The offer surprised Rubin.

"Well?" asked the super.

Rubin was speechless, but the superintendent understood his answer.

"But understand one thing," the super said. "Violate one rule, and I'll ship you out. Got that?"

Rubin got it.

He surprised everyone — guards, staff, other inmates. He made his three months without one rule violation.

When he arrived in the office to pick up his reward — freedom — Superintendent Moore was on vacation. In his place was Mr. Wallace. Rubin claimed to have once found Mr. Wallace sexually abusing a younger inmate. Rubin had beaten the man badly. Mr. Wallace had vowed revenge.

Mr. Wallace handed Rubin a report accusing him of verbal abuse of a staff member. Though unfounded, the report itself would be enough to halt Rubin's promised release.

Rubin, at seventeen, one tough hombre, broke down in tears.

The next night, accompanied by two other inmates, Rubin Carter escaped from Jamesburg State Home by simply walking away.

He embellished the story, and in one version told of ducking bullets and evading vicious farm dogs. However he managed it, two days later, he walked in the front door of his family home in Paterson, New Jersey.

He was home, but he couldn't stay there long.

5

CHAPTER FIVE

BOXING BOAST

Rubin Carter had been drinking the night he offered to fight the best boxers in the U.S. Army in Europe.

An army buddy took Rubin past the hangar where the boxing team worked out. Intrigued, Carter watched for a while.

Cocky by nature and full of beer courage, Rubin loudly proclaimed he could beat any of those — and in his own book used the N word.

His friend turned on Rubin and told him he had a big mouth. He pointed to the coach of the boxing team. "Why don't you tell that guy?"

The friend then steered Rubin until they stood before the coach. "My buddy here thinks he can beat any of your boxers," he said. "He'd like to try out for the team."

The coach and most of the boxing team were regular army. Rubin was a paratrooper. Army regulars resented paratroopers, who were paid more and strutted attitude.

"Come back tomorrow," said the coach. "We'd do it now, but you're drunk and it wouldn't be at all fair."

Rubin had enlisted in the army shortly after his escape from Jamesburg. He had arrived home tired, hungry, ragged, and dirty. He had covered the eighty kilometres (about fifty miles) on foot, evading capture.

The first night at home, his mother fed him, put him in clean clothes, and asked about his plans.

"To join the army," Rubin replied. "Paratroopers."

The goal seemed possible. At seventeen, Rubin was old enough. Looking back, one might question why, after his experience in the military-like school at Jamesburg, he wanted the real thing: discipline, hard work.

But he did. The family bundled him off to relatives in Philadelphia — the same Philadelphia of the *Rocky* movies. At the army recruiting centre, he lied and said he had been raised in Philadelphia (where he would have no police record!).

The army experience only fanned the flames of Rubin's growing sense of anger about the state of blacks in America. The U.S. Armed Forces in 1954 were segregated. Black soldiers served in black units; white soldiers served in white units. It was just like the cottages at

Jamesburg. Black recruits were regularly humiliated with taunts. And, of course, the N word.

But Rubin was in excellent physical shape. He passed all the physical challenges the extra-tough paratrooper training threw his way. He completed basic training and was stationed in Europe.

There, he met his friend Hasson Muhammad, a Muslim. Rubin began to attend a school of Islam and began a spiritual growth that did not flower until almost thirty years later. Muhammad not only introduced Rubin to boxing, but he also showed Rubin, for the first time, the quiet confidence that religion can bring.

Hasson also convinced Rubin that his stutter could be fixed. Rubin still built up anger when he couldn't get the words out. Hasson helped him enroll in speech therapy. Anyone who heard Carter speak later in life, or who has enjoyed his interviews on YouTube and elsewhere, can appreciate the joy that was unleashed.

★   ★   ★

The day after his cocky challenge to the U.S. boxing team, Rubin showed up in borrowed equipment to face the former army heavyweight champion. Heavyweight — a guy twenty or so kilograms (about forty-four pounds) heavier. In the ring it must have looked like a David and Goliath story: Rubin could almost stand under his opponent's chin.

Now sober, Rubin also realized that these boxers were good: trained, conditioned, tough. He realized that boxing in the ring was not the same as street fighting — there were rules, and Rubin Carter didn't much like rules. He was about to go in the ring with a top-notch trained fighter.

He had butterflies.

At the bell, the heavyweight came out bobbing, jabbing, sizing up his smaller target. Rubin ducked and weaved, doing his best to keep out of the bigger man's reach, slipping under that deadly punch. He worked as he would in a street fight.

That may have been his advantage. Conditioned to react to the movements of a trained boxer, the bigger man offered a left hook. Rubin ducked under it, moved as though to go left, came back to the right, and darted back inside.

His first punch of the fight was a blurring left hook that caught the big man on the chin and knocked him down.

But the former champ sprung back to his feet. Rubin pressed his attack, and caught the man with another flurry of blows. Goliath sank to the floor. This time he did not get up.

The crowd that had come to watch the paratrooper get his ass whumped was stunned. Then they broke into cheers.

From that point on, Rubin devoted his time to boxing. He became European Armed Forces weight division champion. He claimed he was invited to the Olympic tryouts in 1956, but would have had to sign up for two more years with the army. He was shipped home in the summer of 1956 when he had finished his two-year stint. Other sources claim he had faced four court martials and was dismissed.

In any event, he ended up back in Paterson, New Jersey, in the summer of 1956. He was ready, he thought, to resume a normal life.

★   ★   ★

On the ocean trip back to America, Rubin had won big at cards — $5,700, he claimed. He plunked down the gambling winnings on a luxury car and clothes. He got a job. A girlfriend.

But Rubin had now seen a much wider world; speech lessons had given him words to express his thoughts. Now he saw Paterson with fresh eyes: dirty streets, run-down housing, an economy beginning a decline. In spite of that, he began to dream of settling down to a life of domestic bliss with his new girl.

Then his past caught up with him.

On the day he planned a picnic with his girlfriend, police crashed into his bedroom and arrested him. He had escaped from Jamesburg; he had to return and do his time.

A year later, twenty-year-old Rubin Carter was released, burning with renewed anger and resentment. By chance he met Little A, the buddy who had fought with him at Jamesburg. They went drinking. His anger spilled into the street. He stole a woman's purse, got in fights for no reason, and beat people. To his dying day, he could not explain why he did this.

He ended up back in prison.

He used his time in prison to build his strength. Running. Push-ups. Strength training. When he emerged four years later, in 1961, he had one goal: to be a professional boxer. Not just *any* pro boxer — champion.

This time, he seemed to be saying, he would use his fists and his anger together legitimately.

For the most part, it worked.

6

CHAPTER SIX

A TITLE SHOT

Rubin Carter's dream of boxing was obviously unrealistic. At twenty-four, he was too old.

He began his career where pro boxers of the day all began: in sleazy, smoke-filled arenas fighting for a few dollars.

His fights were exhibitions: prize fighting. You box, and you get paid. Forty bucks. Sixty bucks. A hundred. That was the game. In his first four months as a pro, Carter fought four fights. He won them all, two by early-round knockouts. He made less than a hundred dollars. Starting at the bottom didn't pay much.

Four years later, Carter had built a strong record. The boxing world had given him a new name. They called him "the Hurricane" for his superior speed and unstoppable power.

His rep now earned him an exhibition match against

welterweight champion Emile Griffith. The Hurricane knocked Griffith out at 2:13 of round one.

It was his thirteenth knockout in twenty-two fights. Could a title shot be far behind?

★   ★   ★

Hurricane Carter met Joey Giardello on December 20, 1964, for the World Middleweight Championship.

Early odds favoured the champion, Giardello, 7–5. But on the day of the bout, betting turned, and Hurricane became the 6–5 favourite.

Experts — if gamblers and bookmakers are experts — thought he would win.

Hurricane, twenty-seven, was a newcomer, three years and three months into a professional career. His spectacular knockout (KO) of Griffith had moved him up the ladder fast.

Giardello was "ring-wise." He was thirty-four years old. He had turned pro at the age of eighteen. In 126 fights, he had lost only twenty-two and delivered thirty-six knockouts. He had won the middleweight championship the year before by defeating Dick Tiger. He was hungry to hold on to the title it had taken him fifteen years to earn. It was his first defence of the title.

The two boxers were evenly matched. Giardello, the champ, weighed in at 72.72 kilograms (160 pounds), and Hurricane, a muscular 71.89 kilograms (158.5 pounds).

The fight was billed as the raw, power-punching newcomer against the wily veteran with boxing smarts. For this fifteen-round title fight, experts predicted that if Giardello could escape Hurricane's powerful punches in the early rounds, his experience would show. Hurricane had never boxed more than ten rounds in any fight.

Could he last?

Hurricane began the pattern for the fight in round one: He pursued the champion, moving relentlessly forward. The champ kept his distance, backing, circling, bobbing, weaving, somehow escaping the wicked punches from Hurricane.

The first three rounds belonged to Hurricane: He carried the fight to the champ, pushing, ever pushing, the champ's only licks coming with counterpunches. Giardello's skills kept him from Hurricane's worst punches; Hurricane swung and missed a lot.

Giardello was passive, reacting to Hurricane's relentless advance. Hurricane showed the energy everyone expected. A flurry by the champion ended round two.

The television commentator noted: "Hurricane has muscles on muscles. Giardello, at thirty-four, has experts wondering if he can last fifteen rounds with Hurricane."

In the fourth round, Hurricane opened a small cut over Giardello's eye. In the middle of the round, he pushed the champ against the ropes. Giardello clung to Hurricane, tying up the challenger to nullify the barrage of fists. With a flurry of blows late in the round, Hurricane deepened the cut over Giardello's eye.

"Make no mistake about it, Hurricane can hit," the announcer told the television audience. "Put two tough fighters together, and you'll have a great fight."

"But Hurricane appears now to be having fun," said another TV commentator. "He is smiling, as though enjoying this bout. And Joey appears to be working harder. At thirty-four, the question of age is important."

At the end of round five, Hurricane reopened the cut over the champ's left eye. In the sixth, Hurricane again threw a series of hard punches at the champ.

The TV announcer said: "They said Hurricane would be able to throw bombs only for four rounds. But here it is in the sixth, and he's still throwing them."

"Giardello seems to be patient," said the colour commentator.

Several times in that sixth round, Hurricane pressed the champ against the ropes. But the champ used his defensive skills to avoid the full power of those blows.

The commentator wondered aloud: "Joey, champ that he is, the class boxer he is, can he hold off this supremely confident, hard-hitting challenger?"

In the seventh, Hurricane continued to take the fight to the champ. "Joey is doing more holding now than he did in the early rounds," the television audience was told, "trying to keep Hurricane at bay and not let him get an open shot with that powerful right hand. Of course, Hurricane also has a blockbuster of a left.

"Anyone who thought Hurricane would run out of steam after four rounds just hasn't seen him lately. He's hardly even breathing hard. He looks as fresh as a daisy."

Both boxers, the commentator insisted, were in the best shape of their careers.

"Joey's wrestling him a lot, trying to wear him down."

In the seventh round, after a flurry in the middle of the ring, the commentator said: "Joey strikes now, and Hurricane is bleeding for the first time. But Joey's looking a little worse for wear. He counters with a heavy blow to the body . . . He's using that jab a lot, but it doesn't seem to have the same power it did in the early rounds."

Round eight: "Hurricane seemed to slow a bit in the seventh; perhaps that blow to the body did it. We could now be at a turning point," said the commentator.

But near the end of the round, he said, "This could

go either way. Neither man has been down."

By the end of round twelve, both fighters were still on their feet. Neither suffered much damage — aside from the cut over the champion's eye in round four. But by now the "experts" had been confounded: Hurricane showed continuing stamina despite the fact he had never been in a bout that lasted this long. The champion by now relied on his ability to cling to his opponent and nullify the sting of attacks.

Before the start of the thirteenth round, the colour commentator suggested that the champion had now to pull together three strong rounds, hinting that Hurricane was ahead on points.

The final two rounds continued the pattern of the whole fight: Hurricane stalked the champion. Giardello continued to elude the challenger, moving in clockwise circles. If Hurricane came close enough to be a danger, Giardello countered with stinging punches of his own.

By the final round, Hurricane knew that in such a close fight, the advantage is to the champion. Challengers must show a clear win to take a title decision. Hurricane had done well, but, many thought, not enough. Perhaps sensing that, Hurricane mounted a last-round flurry. The experts who predicted that he could not last fifteen rounds may have been eating their words. Right to the end, Hurricane pursued the champ. The champ evaded, ducked, moved to his left, circling away.

Despite his best efforts, Hurricane could not find the opening to unleash his powerful right hand.

When the bell sounded, the two boxers almost embraced in a mutual salute.

Forty-five minutes of boxing, and neither fighter had gone down. The cuts the champ had received in the fourth round were the only visible signs of injury.

The boxing crowd buzzed with anticipation after the closing bell. The decision would be up to two judges and the referee.

Hurricane had carried the fight to the champion for the whole night. He pursued Giardello relentlessly, always moving in, the champ always circling back and away. Hurricane sought an opening for a blockbuster; the champion sought a chance for a counterpunch.

Was it enough?

The ring microphone was lowered. The ring announcer read the result:

First judge: Giardello 69, Hurricane 64.

Second judge: Giardello 70, Hurricane 67.

Referee: Giardello 72, Hurricane, 66.

The winner and still Middleweight Champion of the World:

Joey Giardello.

The decision brought both cheers and boos from the crowd, and one disgruntled fan threw an empty bottle into the ring. Hurricane fans were clearly disappointed.

An informal poll of sports writers favoured Giardello by fourteen to seventeen, according to an Associated Press story of the time.

"I won it clear — at least 9–6," said Hurricane, referring to the rounds won by each boxer. "I had him on the hook, but let him get off. He's cagey and takes a helluva punch."

Giardello disagreed. "He fought my fight and didn't press as I expected him to press," Giardello said. "He didn't fight inside and made it easy for me. That had a lot to do with it."

It was Hurricane's only chance at the coveted title.

Private Rubin Carter,
paratrooper, in 1955

The Hurricane
at work in the
ring, December
1963. Carter KO's
Emile Griffith in
the first round.

Lafayette Bar and Grill in Peterson, New Jersey.

CHAPTER SEVEN

BELLO'S STORY

Four months after the shooting at the Lafayette Bar and Grill, Alfred Bello was sitting in his favourite bar when one of his least favourite police officers walked through the door.

Detective Donald LaConte scanned the room quickly. Without hesitation he strode to Bello's table.

"Having a night out?" he asked.

Bello blinked. He wasn't sure where this was leading.

"Okay, relax," the detective said. "This is just an informal chat."

Bello didn't trust "informal chats" with police officers. Even in bars.

"I didn't do nothing," he said.

To the detective, Bello resembled a clown: slicked-back hair, boots with high heels, clothes too tight for even Elvis.

The detective smirked. "I studied grammar in school," he said. "And if you didn't do nothing, then you did do something. What was it?" He pulled out a chair and sat down.

"Huh?"

"Maybe you violated your parole? Yeah, if you did that, you shouldn't tell me."

"I didn't."

"Unless, of course, you had something to give me in return." The detective leaned back in his chair as if to say he wasn't leaving any time soon.

"I'm clean."

"Well, that's good. I'm glad to hear it, Al. But I do need your help. See, I was going over the files on that Lafayette bar shooting. Remember that?"

Bello nodded.

"See, I keep thinking that if I could crack that case, I'd be up for promotion. So anybody who helped me out with that would be my friend. Get my drift?"

Bello again nodded.

"Now you were one of three, maybe four, people who may have seen the killers," said the officer. "You were in the bar right after the shooting, weren't you?"

"Yeah, I called police."

"That's right, that's right. So you are a solid citizen,

doing the right thing. So I'm wondering if there was anything more you've remembered since that night. Anything that could help me. Help me forget about the B & E [break and enter] that took place up the street the same night."

"B & E?"

"At Ace Tool. Funny about that. Never solved, yet you and two friends were nearby at the time. Kellogg. Bradley."

"We didn't . . ."

"Yeah, yeah. Save it for court. I think we've got enough on that one to get your parole revoked. Yes, we do. But if you happened to remember anything more about the shooting . . ."

Bello traced his finger round the draft beer.

"You had the guy," he said, finally. "And you let him go."

"And who would that be?"

"Rubin Carter."

LaConte let that sink in.

"I think you better talk to my boss."

★   ★   ★

Ten days later, Bello found himself led in handcuffs into an interview room. There he met Lieutenant Vince

DeSimone, a detective with the Passaic County prosecutor's office.

The detective looked at Bello with almost friendly eyes.

"Let me take the handcuffs, an' we'll get going," said the big man. "Al Bello, huh?"

Bello nodded.

After his session in the bar with Detective LaConte, Bello had retold his story to Detective Robert Mohl.

"I just, so you know," Mohl said, "Al spoke to us prior, and I told him I'd be goin' to bat for him, but that you're on the county level and want to hear it straight from the horse's mouth."

After some preliminary introductions, DeSimone asked, "How old are you, Al?"

"Twenty-three."

"And your date of birth?"

"Twenty-sixth November, 1943."

"That means this November, this year, you'll be twenty-three. You're really twenty-two now."

"No, twenty-four this November."

The detective tried to correct Bello's math, but gave up rather than anger him. Here was a guy who couldn't figure out his own age.

"So right now you're on parole. When is your parole time?"

"1970." Four more years.

"And who is your parole officer?"

"Mr. Bailey."

"Uh, is this a white man?"

"Coloured."

In the 1960s, the question would have seemed natural. The detective leaned forward as though to confide in the young man.

"You see, why I ask you this, Al. I'm interested in your welfare. This is one of the main reasons we're at Wayne today and not in Paterson. You follow me?"

"Yes."

"I understand you have some information for us. Let me say at the outset, I'm interested in one thing, Al, and that's the truth. You follow me?"

"Yeah."

"In return, I will do everything possible to protect you. Understand?"

"No."

The detective tried to hide his exasperation. "I've heard rumours that you've been threatened. We will do everything possible to protect you up until the time you testify. Following your testimony . . . I can make no definite promises . . . but I will do everything within my power to have your parole transferred to another state."

Bello must have sensed how eager the detective was to hear his story. He came forward with a demand of his own.

"Uh, well, what I was wonderin', uh, if there isn't any way that I could get my parole dropped or somethin'?"

"I can't promise. I'm takin' this a step at a time . . . I understand that you have fear. Of the coloured people an' their supposed movement."

"Yeah."

"I assure you I will go to the top people in the state of New Jersey. I promise you this."

The detective paused.

"About other possible approaches . . . If you were in the area [that night of the shooting] for the possibility of pulling a burglary, there's no evidence that we have of any burglary, even if it were attempted. You understand?"

"Yeah, I understand," Bello replied. Now some of his fears settled down. The cops had brought him in to charge him with the burglary. That would end his parole. Now they were saying this: Give us a good story, and we'll forget the burglary.

The detective continued.

"Now, when we first questioned you, you mentioned Rubin Carter. You said Rubin Carter was the boy."

"Yeah."

The detective then played his trump car.

"The question came up of the money out of the register. And this pulled us poles apart."

Another hidden message: Don't worry about the theft.

Bello told about being in the neighbourhood that night, with his friend Bradley, to break into a building. He was the lookout, or "chickie," whose job it was to "stay on the corner an' watch for police." Even being out on the street at 2:30 a.m. was likely a parole violation. He also may have realized that his being involved in a break-in would not sit well with his parole officer, either.

He said he took a break for a soda when he first saw the white car circling the block.

"I think it was a white, uh, a white Pontiac or a white Chevy at first," said Bello.

"Umm."

"I didn't get a good look at it."

"So the passenger was closest to you."

Bello continued. "I think there was someone sitting in the back seat 'cause I seen, uh, a black figure, you know, black hair. I thought it was a woman or something."

Bello reached for a cigarette. "You don't mind, do you?"

"No, you can smoke. Help yourself."

Bello continued with his story of the car circling the block. Eventually, he continued up the street to the bar to get cigarettes.

"I see a white car parked, right about in, this." He pointed to a photo. "Right about here."

The detective jumped in to help. "It was parked near there, in that vicinity. A white Dodge, right?"

Bello didn't budge. Earlier in the interview, he said the car had been a Chevy or Pontiac. "Well, I don't know if it was a Dodge."

Bello continued with this story.

Lookout duty bored him; after standing on guard for perhaps fifteen minutes longer, he said, he headed to the tavern for cigarettes. A couple of houses from the bar, he heard what he first thought were drums.

He stopped to light up his last cigarette. Now he realized they were shots, Bello said, "'cause I don't think they had a band up there." He continued toward the bar, anyway.

A white car was parked almost in the middle of the street. As he neared it, two men came around the corner carrying guns "laughin', talkin' loud," said Bello. When he got within "ten to fifteen feet" [about five metres], Bello said he realized the men were not detectives, as he first thought. He ran, hiding in the first alley he could find.

Bello saw the two men get into the car. "I heard a car,

like, peeling out, you know, the curb or somethin' . . . so I ran to the front of the alleyway," he said.

Bello continued: "As soon as they passed me, I seen the guy who I had seen at the beginning; I believe it was him, as he turned his head — I mean, like, jammed on the brake, but I guess they changed their mind. You know, they just kept goin' . . . When they jammed on their brakes, I seen the back of the car an', uh, I believe it was a Pontiac, and I said the number quick in my mind, but as fast as I said it, I forgot it."

It was an out-of-town plate; of that he was sure. "New York or Pennsylvania," Bello said.

"And I noticed the back of the car was tapered out." Bello was shown pictures of Hurricane Carter's car.

"Yes, this is definitely the back of the car."

If Bello's memory was sketchy, DeSimone was ready to fill in the missing details: "You identify the back of this car, which bears New York registration 5Z4741, even though you didn't remember the number."

Bello said he then went to the bar, "looked in the door . . . and could see somethin' went down."

"I went back to Bradley and told 'im, you know what I mean?" asked Bello, that the girl upstairs had seen him. (He referred, likely, to Patricia Graham, who lived above the bar. She had looked out her bedroom window to see the two black men get in the car and drive away.)

Bello returned to the bar and entered through the front door. "There was one man sitting in the stool here with his head on the bar. He didn't move."

Another guy got up from his bar stool and wandered around, he said, "but I could see that he was, like, uh, he didn't know whether he was comin' or goin'." This was likely a reference to Willie Marins, the only survivor. "All I see was him walkin' away, like staggerin' away," he said.

"When the girl [Patricia Graham] come in, he was hangin' on to this pole. He had been shot in the head, but he was staggering aroun' the place."

"I said you better stay outside. She didn't stay outside. She walked into the bar. An' screams." Then she left.

Bello said that he saw the bartender face down, behind the bar, a hole in his back. Bello's civic duty was now called: He should call police. "I looked in my pocket for change. I had some quarters. I didn't have no dimes." In those days, pay phone calls cost a dime.

"So I went behind the bar, and I seen that there was money thrown aroun' an', uh, the guy was, like, twisted up back there. I knew he was dead . . . The cash register was open. There was money laying on the floor. So I, uh, took a dime out."

"While I was standing there, I took some of it. I don't

know, it was, it wasn't very much. It was singles. I took some singles . . . maybe twenty-five singles or something like that."

With one thin dime in his pocket, and a fist full of dollars, Bello said, he left the bar, and ran up the street with the money. "I said to Bradley, I said, 'Here.' He says, 'What's this?' So I say, well, uh, I said the bar won't be needin' it anymore. 'Take the f'n money.'"

Bello said he didn't even know how much money there was.

"So there's this woman an' she's bleedin' an' the other guy . . . I figured if I call the police, maybe they'll get there, and maybe they'll save somebody's life." He returned to the bar and called the operator — in those days, you could dial zero and the operator would direct the call. He asked the operator to get him the police.

In the interview, the detectives assured Bello that he would not be charged with anything he had done that night. "I am obliged to tell you by law that you don't have to mention anything that might incriminate you," DeSimone said. "You understand?"

Bello understood.

With some help from detectives, Bello said he was sure the shooters were Hurricane Carter and John Artis.

"Do you know Rubin Carter?" he was asked.

"Prior to this? On the street?"

"I mean, do you know Rubin Carter when you see him?"

"Yeah. Yeah, sure," said Bello.

"Can you tell, uh, whether that was Rubin Carter or wasn't Rubin Carter?"

Bello laughed nervously. "Well, it was Rubin Carter as far as I know or his brother."

The detectives had promised some relief on Bello's parole. They had promised to overlook any crime he may have committed the night of the shooting. He had been brought to the interview in handcuffs. Obviously, he had been arrested for something; although, exactly what was never stated. It is likely at the time that Bello would have told police whatever they wanted to hear as long as it kept him out of jail.

On the other hand, police wanted a conviction badly enough to overlook the holes in Bello's story.

Police didn't bother to see that his timelines made no sense. He was a witness who didn't know how old he was. He couldn't remember a licence plate number — even though he said he was trying to. The story was jumbled, confused, patched together.

Even if he had been earnestly trying to recall the details of that night, he would have had a hard time. By bringing Hurricane and Artis to the scene, the police had set up a situation that could confuse witnesses.

Small details, though, meant little. Police now had a witness who linked Hurricane Carter to the Lafayette triple murder.

★   ★   ★

Three days later, John Artis was home in bed when police smashed through the door. It was the eve of his twentieth birthday.

A shotgun was pressed against his cheek.

"What's the matter?" Artis asked.

"You are being arrested for murder," said one officer.

A high-school athlete, football player, basketball player, track star, Mrs. Artis's son was known as a polite, trouble-free, non-violent kid.

Armed police pushed him roughly down the stairs. His last view of home as a teenager was of his father in the kitchen window, watching as police bundled him into the waiting police car.

That day police also arrested the man they really wanted: Rubin "Hurricane" Carter.

The pro boxer and the teenager were both charged with murder. If found guilty, they faced the death penalty.

8

CHAPTER EIGHT

THE TRIAL

When Hurricane Carter and John Artis were shuffled into the courtroom in April 1967, they had been seven months in custody in the county jail since their arrests in October 1966.

The charges against Hurricane Carter created a press sensation. Prosecutors added to the hubbub by promising a mystery witness.

In the ring, Hurricane Carter's record in ten-round fights was almost even. He won seven, lost eight, and had one draw. The message appeared to be: Stay on your feet against Carter, and you stand an even chance.

Perhaps better than an even chance.

With murder charges hanging over him, Rubin Carter faced the toughest, and longest, fight of his career. He was to go toe-to-toe with the state of New Jersey. The selection of the jury — fourteen members to allow for two spares — took a full two weeks. Even here, racial bias denied equality. One black woman was rejected by the judge because of her limited Grade 6 education; later, the judge refused to reject a white man with only Grade 5 schooling. It was the type of inequality that drove Hurricane into fits of anger.

His defence lawyer was Raymond A. Brown. Artis was represented by a lawyer from the same law firm.

If found guilty, both faced the ultimate knockout — the death penalty.

By today's standards, this trial of a celebrity was quiet. TV cameras weren't allowed in the court; newspaper accounts kept to the facts presented. There were no twenty-four-hour news channel, no shrill voices, no crowds. At its peak the trial drew fewer than seventy-five people — mostly friends and relatives.

The mystery witness turned out to be Alfred Bello.

In the witness stand, Bello repeated the story of being in the area to help with a burglary, and being confronted by two well-dressed and armed black men walking toward him on Lafayette Street. When he realized that the drum sounds he had heard a minute earlier might be more, and that the two men were not detectives, he said, he turned and ran.

The story he told in court was the same one he had

given to the police the previous October. Actually, it was better: His memory had improved.

Now he recalled the sum he took from the cash register: $62. And now the car he saw that night was a Dodge Polara. No doubt at all.

Bello admitted that he had been in the neighbourhood, with his friend Bradley, to break into a building. When it came to his turn to testify, Bradley confirmed the story. They had been dropped off by a third friend, Ken Kellogg. Their goal had been to burglarize the Ace Sheet Metal Company. (Apparently, in spite of police presence and flashing lights until almost dawn, they did manage to pull off that job later that same night.)

Bradley told of seeing the same white car described by Bello. He also told of hearing the same shots. Realizing what this meant, he had sprinted after Bello and now said he had been right behind him when the two black men came around the corner, guns and all, laughing and joking.

According to his story, he spun on his heels and began sprinting back east on Lafayette, and he, too, ducked into the first alley. Or some alley, at least. He told the court that he then talked to Bello, who said he had to return to the bar because he had been seen by some girl in a window.

A few minutes later, he said, Bello returned and shoved part of the wad of bills into his hands — his split.

When he counted it later, he said, it was $62.

Patricia Graham, now Patricia Valentine since her wedding, told her story of seeing "two Negro men run to a white car with out-of-state licence plates" after hearing big bangs coming from the tavern.

All three witnesses — Bello, (Graham) Valentine, and Bradley — gave testimony about the car. A white car that from the back, they said, "lit up like a butterfly." A police officer had made sketches the night of the shooting based on Valentine's description, but those sketches had been thrown away.

The description of the car tail lights should have caused confusion. Dodge had two models that year with similar rear-end looks. There was one difference. The Dodge Monaco had tail lights and brake lights that spread out almost across the whole back of the vehicle, wide on the outside, narrower in the middle. In daylight, the Dodge Polara looked similar — except the rear lights were only on the outside corners, not all the way across. Chrome markers outlined the same trunk lid, but the trunk lid did not light up as did the Monaco's.

The brake lights of the Monaco did, indeed, "light up like a butterfly." Carter's car was a Polara — and did not.

The third of the infamous burglary trio was Ken Kellogg. At the time, Kellogg had been the designated driver for the burglary. He dropped off Bello and Bradley, and then parked a block away to wait.

Kellogg said he waited for a while, felt thirsty, so walked around the block to the Lafayette bar. He had hoped to find someone he knew who would buy him a drink. There were four or five people in the bar at the time, he said. No one bought him a drink, so he returned to his car, and was stretched out in the back seat when the shooting occurred.

Kellogg said when he heard police sirens, he realized his car was getting a flat tire. He drove to a gas station to pump it up.

He also admitted to returning to the sheet metal company later that morning with Bradley. This time they did get in, he said.

Defence lawyer Brown tried to point out that Kellogg's testimony was not reliable. He had, Brown claimed, given slightly different stories to police and at the Grand Jury hearing.

Superior Court Judge Samuel Larner wouldn't allow it. He directed Brown to just "question the witness."

Police witnesses also testified about picking up spent shotgun shells in the bar after the killing. One officer also said that the morning of the shooting, he searched Carter's car. He reported finding a live 12-gauge shotgun shell, a live .32-calibre cartridge, and a handgun in the car. The shooting was done with a 12-gauge shotgun and a .32-calibre handgun.

The same officer testified that he had shown the ammunition to both Valentine and to a reporter at the time. However, he admitted he had not logged the items in the evidence lab until five days later.

The trial itself lasted a full two weeks. In the end, defence produced character witnesses for Artis and two women — Cathy McGuire and her mother — who said Carter drove them home about the time the murders were committed.

Even John "Bucks" Royster was called to testify. Royster was the front-seat passenger when Carter's car was first stopped that night. Royster couldn't seem to resist a drink. In court, he slouched in his seat. Judge Larner asked, "How many drinks have you had this morning?"

"I don't know," Royster replied.

Boiled down to essentials, the prosecutor laid out a possible schedule: Carter and Artis had committed the crime, then had jumped in their car and sped off. The theory said they had dumped the guns at the house of

Eddie Rawls, picked up Royster somewhere, and were crossing Broadway at 127th Street — not speeding — when police pulled them over the first time. This was ten to twelve minutes after the shooting.

The defence story was simpler: With Artis driving, Carter had left the Nite Spot and was heading home for more cash when he was picked up. Two witnesses testified Carter was driving them home shortly after 2:00 a.m., about the time of the shooting.

On May 26, 1967, the jury filed out to make a decision.

If found guilty, the two faced the death penalty. It was a heinous crime. To add passion to the case, the prosecuting lawyer held up blood-soaked clothing to emphasize the horror of the crime.

The prosecutor claimed that John Artis had emptied a handgun at a fifty-one-year-old grandmother at point-blank range. He had shot two men in the head. Carter was accused of blasting a shotgun shell into the back of the bartender, Jimmy Oliver, and another into the chest of a grandmother.

For five hours and thirty-five minutes, Hurricane and Artis waited nervously. Finally, the jury filed back.

"Do you have a verdict?" asked the judge.

"We do," said the jury foreman.

"Will the defendants please rise?"

John Artis and Rubin "Hurricane" Carter stood.

For John Artis, it was a scene from a horror movie. His heart pounded as though it would burst from his chest. It was the most afraid he had been in his life.

"Please read the verdict," said the judge.

The foreman held a piece of paper before him. The courtroom fell silent. Hurricane hardly dared to breath. Boxing has its judges called referees, and he had been on the bad end of a bad decision before.

He waited.

Then:

"We find both men guilty on all three counts of murder in the first degree."

Hurricane had once sparred with Sonny Liston. He had felt the power of one of the heaviest fists in boxing history. It was nothing to what he felt at that moment.

But as the judgment sucked the air from his lungs, he heard the rest of the sentence:

"With a recommendation for life imprisonment."

It seemed as though the jury felt they had to find them guilty, but weren't quite sure.

CHAPTER NINE

LIFE IN PRISON

Hurricane Carter had spent four years in Trenton State Prison ten years earlier. He knew the routines. He knew the dangers and politics of life in prison.

Prison swallowed the souls of both the inmates and the guards. In theory, people are put in prison for three reasons: first, to take them off the street so they cannot harm others; second, to give them skills so that when released they will function as good citizens.

Third, as punishment.

In the six years he had been free after his first prison term, he had climbed to the top rungs of the boxing world. He had a title bout. Now he returned to what he could describe only as a hellhole. In those six years, he had fulfilled his dream of becoming a professional boxer. He had not only succeeded, he had been one of the best in the world. He knew now he could someday be a world champ.

He couldn't do that in prison.

His goal: to prove his innocence, get out of jail, and resume his boxing career.

First, though, he had to stay alive. He knew that prison could suck the dignity out of any man.

His first act was to refuse to wear prison clothes. He also declared that he would refuse any prison make-work jobs. He refused to eat prison food. He had a friend, Thom Kidrin, bring him food that he kept in his cell.

While the prison could contain his body, he was essentially saying that prison could not contain his spirit, his soul, his dignity.

He announced to prison staff that no one must ever lay a hand on him. He had seen what guards could and would do to make a prisoner conform. He had also seen what prisoners could and would do to each other in fights, beatings, and stabbings. By declaring his own no-touch policy for guards, he also sent a message to other inmates: hands off.

The defiance brought the expected response: He was taken to solitary confinement.

In his first book, *The Sixteenth Round,* Carter said that in his first days back in Trenton, he had the equivalent of a team meeting involving Rubin, Hurricane, and Carter. His description of these three parts of his personality is interesting. Rubin, he said, was the thoughtful one. Rubin wanted to study law and find out what went wrong, and what could be done get him (them?) out of jail. Carter, introverted, quiet, wanted to write a book to tell the world about the injustice. Hurricane — the part of him that unleashed fury in the boxing ring — was the angry one. He raged at the injustice done to him; raged against the treatment of blacks in the U.S.; raged over the riots then ripping through U.S. society; raged over the murder and beatings of civil rights advocates; raged, still, in some small part of his being, at the beatings his father had given him.

It was Hurricane who warned prison officials to keep hands off: If someone touched Rubin Carter, it would be Hurricane who fought back. An angry Hurricane.

In solitary confinement, Rubin and Carter came to an agreement with Hurricane. "One thing was accepted by us all," he wrote. "And that was we would definitely not submit to this prison's nastiness. We would study the law (Rubin) and write this book (Carter), and if that didn't work, then let the Hurricane take over and do what must be done."

Rubin "Hurricane" Carter was now a focused angry man. Like a Transformers toy, he was willing to appear first as a mild and scholarly writer. But at the right moment, his anger could transform him into a trained fighting machine.

★   ★   ★

He began by studying the law. Lawyers say that anyone who acts as his own lawyer has a fool for a client. Rubin's lawyer wouldn't answer his letters. He would not send a copy of the trial transcript. Nevertheless, with the help of another inmate, he began to study his own case in detail.

Street understanding of the law is based on how police apply certain aspects of it. The law, as written, is often different. The law, he discovered, is both the written law and how courts interpret that law.

Now that he had been convicted, the law no longer cared if he was innocent. Courts would overturn his conviction only if he had been given an unfair trial, if his rights had been violated, or if the judge made wrong rulings.

He learned that the search of his car was illegal. He and Artis were brought to the scene of the murders. A crowd milled about. Anyone could have planted shotgun cartridges and live bullets in his car. Worse, Carter was not present when the car was searched.

The police officer who did the search said he had

found a live shotgun cartridge and a .32-calibre bullet in the car. He showed these to a news reporter and to Valentine — but did not record the findings until five days later. A common principle in such matters is continuity of evidence. The live ammo claimed to have been in Hurricane's car was stuck in a desk drawer for five days. The officer could not prove that the items he finally booked in the evidence room were the ones he found — if, indeed, he had found any.

Hurricane also discovered a gap in the *Miranda* clause. The *Miranda* warning is one familiar to anyone who watches cop shows on TV. "You are under arrest for X charge. You have the right to remain silent. Anything you do say can and will be used against you in a court of law. You have the right to retain counsel . . ."

The *Miranda* entered U.S. law only in May 1966, the month before the shootings. It was new to both police and lawyers. But the fact was clear: Carter had been given no warning the night he was picked up and questioned.

In addition, Hurricane Carter also thought that the sloppy police investigation might be enough to free him. Police had not fingerprinted the bar. They took no official statements from witnesses aside from notes by officers typed up after the event. Worse, they had brought

Carter and Artis back to the scene, needlessly confusing the memory of witnesses.

To him it seemed obvious that Valentine had confused her memory of the white car she had seen fleeing the scene with her memory of Carter's car.

He knew that both Bello and Bradley had lied. He suspected that police had offered them a deal to lie on the stand. But how could he prove that? Maybe Bello and Bradley had overheard Patricia describing the car to police.

He even doubted the effectiveness of his own lawyer. Carter thought that Brown should have asked to have the trial moved to another county. He said the "highly publicized accounts of a racially motivated triple murder of white citizens by two Negroes made it impossible . . . to receive a fair trial in Paterson."

And the jury: The law is supposed to guarantee a hearing before a jury of peers. To Hurricane, that meant a jury made up of a sampling of people from his community. He had friends both white and black. Paterson, a city of 120,000, had a black population of 35,000. That is a ratio of about three to one.

Yet the jury had one black person on the panel of fourteen. When it came time to whittle the jury down to the final twelve who would make the decision, that black man was dismissed. Carter thought the jury should have included at least three black people. His peers.

Carter brought all of his findings to the Supreme Court of New Jersey. He thought any of his allegations would have been grounds for at least a new trial.

In July 1969, the Supreme Court ruled:

"It is fair to say that the case had to turn upon the State's proof and the defendants' denial of guilt, unaided by the testimony which sought to establish incompatible presence elsewhere . . ."

In other words, it boiled down to he-said, she-said. Who you gonna believe? The Supreme Court believed the prosecution:

"The judgments are therefore affirmed."

His appeal denied, Rubin began to shrivel. Hurricane was warming up in the corner of the ring, his scowling face under a hoodie. On visiting day, he sat and cried with his wife, Mae Thelma, and his daughter, Theodora, until they left. Hours later he was still sitting there, alone.

The reality, the hopelessness, began to sink in.

10

CHAPTER TEN

ENTER THE STARS

His appeal denied, Hurricane Carter began some of his darkest days in prison. Hope came in a form he had not expected.

A visitor showed up at Rahway Prison, where Carter had been transferred.

His name was Fred Hogan. Years before, Hogan had been a young boxer who had visited Hurricane Carter's training camp. Hurricane had autographed a fight poster. Hogan had treasured the poster and took it with him when he served in the army. He displayed it proudly.

During Hurricane's trial, Hogan was in the U.S. Army in Europe. His father sent him press clippings so he could follow the case. When the guilty verdict was announced, Hogan was shocked. He didn't believe that his hero could commit such a horrible murder.

After Hogan got out of the army, he became a police

officer, and then an investigator for the public defender's office. His job took him into prisons, where he interviewed prisoners.

On one such visit to Rahway Prison, he decided on a whim to drop in on Hurricane Carter. Hurricane did not remember Hogan. No wonder. A decade had added pounds to Hogan's frame, and he looked even older, softer, not the young boxer Hurricane had met.

Besides, Hurricane was wary. He trusted no one.

The visit did not go well.

"I don't believe you're guilty, man," Hogan said.

Hurricane simply shrugged.

But Hogan would not be put off.

"Okay, then," he said. "But if I want to prove you didn't do it, where would I look?"

Hurricane looked up at his visitor. No one had asked that before.

He replied curtly: "Bello and Bradley."

Hurricane didn't really believe Hogan would follow up. Everybody talks a good fight, he had found, but aren't around when the going is tough.

By now, Hurricane had begun his study of the law. At all hours, he was busy in his cell typing away one finger at a time on a book that would eventually become *The Sixteenth Round*.

Fred Hogan surprised him. He tracked down both Bradley and Bello.

Hogan first visited the site of the Ace Sheet Metal Company, where Bradley had been using his trusty tire iron to break in. From where Bradley had said he stood, he could not have seen the white car with two black men in it.

Hogan tracked Bradley down. Bradley admitted to lying at the trial.

Bello took longer to find. Hogan finally tracked him down: He was in jail.

Bello, too, said he had lied at the trial. He could not identify the two men that night. Bello also believed that his testimony was the key to Carter's conviction. He had even made an official application for the reward ($10,500), but had been told to wait until Carter's appeal had been dealt with — and then never received the money.

Bello was in jail, facing more criminal charges. He felt that Detective DeSimone had not kept his part of the bargain.

Separately, both Bello and Bradley signed statements admitting they had lied. Both repeated their story to Selwyn Raab of *The New York Times* and Richard Solomon, the TV producer.

In 1974, *The Sixteenth Round* was published. Raab

wrote a detailed story of the case in *The New York Times*.

Hurricane sent a copy of his book to folk rock star Bob Dylan. Dylan, a popular singer and composer, had been the poet of the youthful revolution of the 1960s: flower children, civil rights. His song "The Times They Are A-Changin'" had motivated a social revolution at the time.

Dylan wrote Carter's story in the song "Hurricane." The ballad was released on an album about the same time Hurricane Carter's appeal was before the Supreme Court of New Jersey.

An advertising man planned a campaign to bolster support for Hurricane and raise funds for his legal defence. He recruited stars of sports and entertainment to Hurricane Carter's fight for justice. This included boxer "Smokin' Joe" Frazier, National Baseball Hall of Famer Hank Aaron, Hollywood stars Dyan Cannon, Ellen Burstyn, and Burt Reynolds, as well as singing stars Roberta Flack and Harry Belafonte.

Coretta Scott King, wife of slain civil rights champion Martin Luther King, Jr., Rev. Jesse Jackson, and others joined in.

The list grew. Hurricane Carter became the poster boy for injustice.

Muhammad Ali's support led the way. In 1967, when

drafted into the U.S. Army to serve in the Vietnam War, Ali had refused. He said he had "no fight with the Viet Cong." As a result, he had been stripped of his heavyweight championship and sentenced to jail. He felt strongly about injustice.

The year 1975 was Hurricane's year. The stars were on his side. Dylan's song "Hurricane" topped the music charts. With Bello and Bradley changing their story, another hearing was granted. Hurricane was released on parole.

In October of that year, Carter's case went before Judge Samuel Larner, the original trial judge. Judge Larner listened to the new stories presented by Bradley and Bello.

But Judge Larner ruled that their change of story "lacked the ring of truth." Follow this logic: When the liars lied at the trial, Judge Larner believed them; when they admitted they had lied, the judge thought they were . . . lying. Go figure.

Like a jab to the nose, the judgment hurt. But it was not a knockout punch. Instead, it allowed Carter's team to go inside and counterpunch.

In the process of preparing for Larner's hearing, the prosecutor's office revealed that a recording had been made of Bello's interview with DeSimone.

Hurricane's lawyers thought the tape showed that Bello had been asked leading questions and given promises of leniency. They thought the police had bribed Bello for the right testimony. Using this, the case was referred to the Supreme Court.

The interview had taken place four months after the murders at the Lafayette. At the time, Bello faced other charges. He was already on parole and could expect that parole to be revoked. He faced prison.

DeSimone clearly promised to overlook the theft of cash from the till at the Lafayette, and the break-in at the Ace Sheet Metal Company. Bello had asked if his parole could be lifted, and was promised that it might be moved to another state.

The interview showed that DeSimone's offers of protection and the leading questions were subtle. Hurricane's lawyers argued that Carter had been denied a fair trial.

On appeal, Judge Larner had not thought so.

But Judge Larner's ruling meant little. What was important was that this new information allowed an appeal to the Supreme Court of New Jersey.

Once again, Hurricane Carter found himself waiting in suspense for the referees' decision.

When it came, it was unanimous: The judges ruled 7-0. Hurricane Carter had not been treated fairly. His conviction was set aside. He would be granted a new trial.

Muhammad Ali stepped forward and provided bail for both Carter and Artis, and a roll of bills to live on. For the first time in ten years, Hurricane Carter was free — almost.

The two key witnesses, Bello and Bradley, had recanted. The second trial would be a formality, and then both Carter and Artis would be free.

Right?

11

CHAPTER ELEVEN

THE SECOND TRIAL

It had taken ten years, but Rubin Carter — and John Artis — were nearing victory.

Public support had been strong.

The second trial was seen by most as a formality. The two key witnesses, Bello and Bradley, had changed their testimony.

Concerts in Madison Square Garden and the Astrodome in Houston, Texas, were held to raise money for their defence fund. Pop stars of the day lined up to perform.

However, just as the sun appeared to be shining brightly for both men, dark clouds moved in.

The concerts didn't pan out well. Even though a whole list of stars performed for free, the sold-out concert at Madison Square Garden raised only $100,000 — half of the revenues. The Astrodome concert ticket sales totalled almost $400,000 — and lost money.

Rubin argued with some who had been strong supporters. Many were now to find that a fight with Rubin
was a fight to the finish. A promoter pocketed money
from the defence fund. He was dismissed. Richard
Solomon, the TV producer, was also dismissed.

Even life on the home front soured. Rubin's wife,
Mae Thelma, had visited him weekly in prison for ten
years. She had even lived on welfare. Now, she had
hoped that with Carter free on parole, they would spend
time together. Rubin's attention, though, focused on his
defence. He needed money, and now his only source of
income lay in speaking engagements. Rubin had left his
stutter far behind. Universities, colleges, and professional
groups paid well to hear his inspiring story — the steps
to righting an injustice. Speaking meant travel, and travel
meant time away from home.

Then entered another woman: Carolyn Kelley.

Kelley had visited Carter in prison. At the suggestion
of a cousin, she had been involved in organizing fundraising rallies for Rubin.

After Rubin had been put on parole and was await-
ing his second trial, he and Kelley became romantically
involved.

The romance ended when she accused Carter of
beating her.

Kelley said the incident happened when she visited his hotel room in Maryland after a Muhammad Ali fight on April 29, 1967. She said that Carter hit her hard enough to knock her out, and then beat her black and blue. However, she did not report the beating until six weeks later. On June 7, she held a press conference, claiming that Carter had tried to kill her.

Carter pointed out that Kelley never laid charges. Prosecutors demanded that Carter's parole end and his $20,000 bail bond be forfeited. The bail hearing revealed that Kelley had sought treatment at three different hospitals in two days after the incident in what seemed to be an attempt to find a doctor who saw bruises.

Carter claimed Kelley had sought payment for her fundraising efforts. He said they had quarrelled, but he had never hurt her. Because the accusations proved flimsy, Carter remained free on bail.

However, the damage to Carter's reputation had been done. Support from celebrities fell off. By the time of his second trial in fall 1976, even some of his family had given up. His wife was pregnant, his lover had accused him of physical abuse, and even supporters seemed to want bits and pieces of him.

His second trial lasted five weeks.

By this time, Rubin Carter should not have been surprised by anything. But he was.

Alfred Bello, who had admitted he had lied at the first trial, changed his story again. When he said he had lied, he now told the court, he was lying. It seemed to be all he ever did.

Bello was a small-time crook, burglar, thief, and liar. His plumpish figure he now adorned with outlandish clothes. James Hirsch, a reporter with *The New York Times* and author of *Hurricane,* said he appeared at the trial dressed in ". . . a tight suit, red cowboy boots, he chewed gum or candy, belched," and spoke like someone out of a 1950s TV drama.

In the second trial, Bello returned to his original story: He identified Carter and Artis as the two men he had seen by the bar with weapons. Not only that, his memory had improved. In his original statement (October 11, 1966) to DeSimone, he couldn't be sure he could identify Artis. Now he was sure, and claimed that he had told police the night of the shooting.

This was an interesting turn of events. No other witness or police testimony suggested any identity of Carter or Artis that night. If it were true, though, why would police have released both Carter and Artis from custody?

Bello wasn't finished. He said Fred Hogan offered

him cash to say he had lied at the first trial. He said the money came from the advance on royalties from Rubin's book *The Sixteenth Round*.

In just a few months, Bello had gone from feeling cheated out of the $10,500 reward money to saying that Carter's team had bribed him to lie.

Bello was not the only witness with improved memory. Patricia (Graham) Valentine, the young mother with the apartment right over the Lafayette Bar, now told the trial that on the night of the shooting, a police officer had shown her the live ammo supposedly found in Carter's car. At the first trial, Carter's car was similar to the white getaway car "with butterfly lights." Now, she said, it was not just similar. It was *definitely* the car.

Two defence witnesses, Cathy McGuire and her mother, also changed their stories. At the original trial, both said that Carter had driven them home that evening. This provided a perfect alibi for the time of the shootings. Now both said they had lied because Carter had asked them to lie.

The jury, this time with two black members, took nine hours, including lunch and dinner, to come to a verdict.

After the verdict, Carter held his newborn son Raheen for the first and only time.

Shortly after, he divorced Mae Thelma.

Carter and Artis were again found guilty of murder in the first degree, and sentenced again to the same life sentences as from the first trial.

12

CHAPTER TWELVE

```
THE HOLE IN THE WALL
```

On his return to Trenton State Prison, Rubin Carter was asked for his prisoner identity card. He bristled.

"My name is Rubin Carter," he told the guard. "I don't need an ID card."

When he was summoned for work duty, he told the guard, "I don't have time."

It was a pattern that Rubin had followed before. He refused to follow prison rules. He wore his own clothes. He continued to refuse prison food. It was the only way he knew of not becoming a prison zombie, unable to survive outside of prison.

Prison officials did not see it that way. As an example to other prisoners, he was charged by the attorney general over his refusal to conform.

He wrote back, citing case law: "I have no time for anything except fighting for my freedom!"

Guards who did not know his background sometimes ran afoul of Rubin's law: No guard was to touch Rubin Carter under any circumstance. James Hirsch tells of one rookie guard who found Rubin asleep and reached inside the cell and tapped his ankle.

Rubin responded that if he want to keep breathing, he should keep his hands to himself. His language was a bit more flowery and not fit for young readers.

One hot day in June 1977, Rubin strolled in the prison yard with another man. He was now a long way from the ten-mile runs of his boxing days. He wasn't used to walking. Exhausted, he sat down to rest in the shade against the wall.

"As I leaned against the wall, I looked across the yard at the opposite wall, a thirty-six-foot [eleven-metre] brick wall," he wrote in his final autobiography, *The Eye of the Hurricane.* ..."I was just staring at the wall and something strange began to happen. I rubbed my eyes because I could not believe what I was seeing. A pinprick of light was coming through that solid wall. As I stared at the light, it began to quiver and grow bigger and bigger. Eventually, I could see through the wall! I could see cars passing by in the street. I could see schoolchildren coming back from classes."

He thought he was hallucinating. The hole disappeared.

But that mystical hole in the wall told him that the path to freedom from prison lay not in the law, but in the spirit. A triumph of the spirit would melt prison bars and walls.

With a Grade 8 education, he had studied law, directed lawyers, written a book. His boxing career had created Hurricane Carter, the tough guy who loved night life, booze, and women. Convicted of a crime he did not commit, he became a law student, a writer, an advocate for himself. Rubin, the law student, and Carter, the writer, had kept Hurricane under control.

Could Hurricane be contained? What did he need now to retain his sense of self, his dignity, his sanity? Was there more about Rubin Carter than boxer, lawyer, writer?

He turned inward. He decided he needed to find himself.

In his first term in Trenton State — before his boxing career — he had prepared himself physically. He had run, long and hard, in the prison yard. He had done push-ups — an impossible 5,000 before breakfast, he once said. He had developed his physique so he would be ready for the boxing career he knew would bring him glory.

In his second term, those ten years, he had lost an eye to a botched medical procedure, a wife, and family, but had read law long and hard, had written a book, clicking one typewriter key at a time. He had prepared for the second trial that he felt would bring vindication.

He had lost.

Now he prepared for a more important battle. He gave away his law books. He asked his one loyal friend, Thom Kidrin, to bring him different books, along with food.

Not books about boxing or other sports. Not trite detective stories, nor westerns, nor even romances, nor fantasy to escape — no fiction at all.

Big books. Meaningful books.

Books by philosophers who had thought long and deeply about the meaning of life. By people like Einstein, Plato, Socrates, Krishnamurti, Frankl, Nietzsche, Zola, Gurdjieff, Ouspensky, Velikovsky.

He read the Bible, both the Old Testament and the New Testament; the Quran, the Bhagavad-Gita, and Kabbalah.

The same determination that had built his body in strength and toughness, he now applied to his soul and his mind.

He set out to discover who Rubin Carter *really* was.

13

CHAPTER THIRTEEN

LESRA'S LETTER

It was a letter from a sixteen-year-old black teen from Toronto, Canada, that changed Hurricane's life.

At the time, Hurricane had stacks of unopened letters under his bunk. He had stopped responding to fan mail. And to hate mail. He got more than his share of that, too.

Perhaps the childlike handwriting attracted him.

Lesra Martin, sixteen, lived in Toronto. He was originally from New York. He had written to Rubin Carter because he had read the book *The Sixteenth Round*, and had seen parallels between himself and Carter.

Lesra was living a storybook fantasy.

Lesra grew up in New York. He had lived in a run-down ghetto next to drug dealers and gangs. He was one of eight children. His parents were on welfare. Both had drinking problems.

The summer he was fifteen, Lesra worked in a government laboratory as an intern paid for by the city. It was the ideal summer job. He was bright, articulate, and a top student in his high-school class. He was five-feet-nothing tall and full of play, had poor eyesight, a runny nose, and a chipped front tooth.

At this summer job, Lesra met a strange group of Canadians who took an interest in him.

The three Canadians were in New York on a business trip: Lisa Peters, the leader; Terry Swinton; and Itel Renbaum.

Lesra and a friend worked in the lab that summer. Their duties were not clearly spelled out. The two spent a lot of their time in horseplay. While washing cars, they would often hose each other down. Lesra began to chat up this strange group of Canadians.

Lesra had grown up in a black neighbourhood and spoke "black English," which, at times, the Canadians found difficult to understand. It was almost, to them, another language.

Despite the language barrier, the three grew to like Lesra. One day they offered him a ride home from the lab. Lesra lived with his family in a fourth-floor walk-up in a condemned building shared with seven other families. The family apartment had no locks on the doors and only two windows, one of which was never opened summer or winter. The neighbourhood showed a level of poverty that the Canadians found hard to believe. On the streets were mattresses and derelict cars. Windows and doors were boarded shut. Most buildings were in dire need of repair.

Lisa Peters, the leader, had herself grown up in a form of poverty with an abusive father. Her mother had died in childbirth. Peters left home at fourteen and lived on the streets. Pregnant at seventeen, she married, but it didn't last. She joined a group in a commune, and now, years later, the commune had become a business operation. Their home in Toronto was a large, well-furnished house with a large yard.

Peters had a son almost the same age as Lesra. The poverty they saw in New York was shocking. They wondered if they could do something for Lesra.

That summer, Lesra was invited to Toronto for a visit during Caribana — an annual Caribbean festival held the first weekend in August. The colour and the excitement captivated him, as did the quiet of Toronto. Compared to New York, he found it peaceful. Once, he was tapped on the shoulder by a police officer. His offence? He had dropped a candy wrapper on the street. In the streets of Toronto he found little of the racism, mistrust, and hatred that ruled his part of New York.

Lesra had plans to become a lawyer. He had no idea of the education, hard work, or cost. He did know that lawyers made good money, and among the people he knew, lawyers were more in demand than plumbers.

By the summer's end, he had charmed the Canadians, who then made a big pitch. Would Lesra's parents consent to his moving to Toronto for an education?

It was a big step: to move a child to a foreign country, with strangers, people they knew little about. Lesra's father, Earl Martin, accepted a visit to Toronto to check out the conditions. The commune paid his plane fare.

Earl Martin was surprised at the relative luxury of the Toronto home. The Canadians, in turn, were surprised at his claim to have been a lead singer for the singing group the Del Vikings, which had several hits songs in the 1950s.

Lesra's parents agreed. They could see that this would be the one chance for their son to escape the life of poverty and crime that ruled the ghetto. Besides, it would be one less mouth to feed. Lesra moved from New York to Toronto.

At first, Peters and the commune planned to enrol Lesra for school that fall. He should have been going into Grade 11.

Lesra was bright and very articulate. He had stood near top of his class in New York.

Then came an almost shocking discovery.

Lesra could not read.

He had memorized the shape of some words, and had become good at guessing others. But he had no skills at figuring out new words. His math skills were also weak.

Having missed the skills, Lesra also missed content. He had no idea of what country he had grown up in. He had no concept of country at all. Though each day he had recited the Pledge of Allegiance to the Flag of the United States of America, he had no idea what was meant by pledge, allegiance, or even the United States. Geography. History. Science. He had missed it all.

Perhaps worse was that Lesra had thought that black people could not learn.

Peters's son, Marty, was almost the same age. When he was eight, Marty had been diagnosed with dyslexia. This is a reading disability that mixes up letters. He had been home-schooled. That had been a success.

But now the goal was to prepare Lesra for university. The group knew that Lesra was bright and articulate. That he had not learned did not mean he could not learn. He just needed the opportunity.

Lesra's education began.

First he was given new clothes, dental care, and health care that cured his runny nose. For the first time, he began to eat properly.

To learn to read, he had to, well, read. They had to find books that would interest him, in spite of his weak reading skills. He wouldn't learn to read with books that bored him.

They took him to a used book sale held by the Toronto Public Library. Lesra found a book that caught his interest. It was *The Sixteenth Round: From Number 1 Contender to Number 45472* by Rubin "Hurricane" Carter. He paid a quarter for it.

Lesra's older brother had spent time in prison. In his early schooling, Lesra had thought that black people were not smart. Now, he had a book written by a black man.

He liked it so much, he wrote to the author.

Lesra had worked hard on the letter. Others in the commune had helped edit it, and Lesra revised it several times.

In part it said:

> The thought of writing you scared me, but not because of your reputation — I know you wouldn't hurt a flea (unless it bit you). I feel frightened and vulnerable because I have to see you now not just as an author, but as a human being. It is hard at the

best of times for black people to open up to each
other because where we come from, you learn to
be tough when you learn to walk.

... My eldest brother did time up state in New
York ... Since I read your book, I can understand
him and his problems a whole lot better. You were
not only asking someone to help you through
your book, you were also helping others.

... Hey, Brother, I'm going to let it go here. Please
write back. It will mean a lot.

Your friend,
Lesra Martin.

And that is the letter that Rubin Carter opened that day.

14

CHAPTER FOURTEEN

FREE AT LAST

Lesra's letter played a tune on Rubin Carter's heart.

Rubin saw right away the similarities. Both he and Lesra were black. Both had grown up with racism. But here was a black kid who was being given a chance to escape.

Rubin wrote back. The letters led to phone calls and finally to a visit.

The story of Rubin Carter and Lesra Martin is worth a whole book in itself. In fact, a book has been written. In the book *Lazarus and the Hurricane,* Sam Chaiton and Terry Swinton, two members of the Toronto commune who adopted Lesra, tell the story in detail.

Lesra's visit with Rubin in prison was just the beginning. Several of the members of the commune moved to New Jersey to be near Rubin, and took a strong interest in his case.

Meanwhile, the lawyers continued the fight.

By now, Rubin's strategy lay completely in process. He knew that the process demanded that he first use all of the appeal possibilities at the state level. Once that was exhausted, he might qualify for an appeal to the federal courts, and there he might have a better chance.

Meanwhile, John Artis was freed on parole on December 22, 1982. He was thirty-six.

In prison, Artis had four toes on one foot amputated. Later, he lost several fingers to the same disease that doctors said was made worse by the cold and damp of prison. One car ride had cost him his youth, his ambitions for a track scholarship, and sixteen years.

In that time, Artis had stuck by Rubin's side. Before the second trial, prosecutors suggested that Artis and Carter be tried separately — and if Artis agreed, they hinted that they would not follow through with charges against Artis. It had to have been a tempting offer, but it meant deserting his friend. Other times, Artis was promised freedom if he would admit that he and Carter were guilty.

He would not change his story, and had been a model prisoner. He had met a woman, married, and now was free — or as free as parole allows.

Meanwhile, Rubin Carter, through his lawyers, continued his fight for freedom.

Before the second trial, Alfred Bello told prosecutors in private that he was *inside the bar* at the time of the shooting.

This was, indeed, a new twist. Bello claimed that at the time of the shooting, he had hidden behind Hazel Tanis and escaped unharmed. This was a strange story. Many later thought Bello had invented it so he could sell the story as a book or movie.

In this version, Bello apparently claimed that Carter and Artis were lookouts outside the bar and definitely were not the killers.

If the story were true, it would have cleared Carter and Artis.

Before the second trial, Bello had been given a lie detector test. The technician who gave the test provided a report that said Bello's story at the first trial was the truth.

Lie detector tests can't be used in court. But here was a quirk: Rubin's lawyers at the second trial had not been told of the test. The courts insisted on disclosure: Police have to share information with the defence lawyers.

Likely because the "inside-the-bar" story was hard to believe, prosecutors asked Bello to repeat the story from his first trial.

Four years after the second trial, defence learned of the Bello lie detector test. Rubin's lawyer, Myron

Beldock, thought something seemed strange. He phoned the technician who gave the test.

The technician stuck by his guns; he said Bello was telling the truth when he said he was inside the bar.

"But your report said that he told the truth at the first trial."

"Yes," answered the technician.

"At the first trial," Beldock told him, "Bello said he was on the street, not in the bar."

"Oh."

If you made up stuff like this, no one would believe it.

So here we have a lie detector test report, which can't be used in court, confusing a lie with true testimony. But the report couldn't be used, anyway. But since the prosecutors hadn't told the defence that the test had been given, then Carter's right to a fair trial had been denied.

That was the argument Rubin's lawyers made.

Who said law was simple?

It really didn't matter. By the time of an appeal hearing in 1981, Bello's mind had been so blotted by years of drinking and drugs that he said he could not recall the night of the shooting, the story he told police, or even his testimony in either trial.

Having discovered the hornswoggle, Carter used this

confusion to appeal on the basis that he had not been given a fair trial.

He lost.

But this time, it was a split decision; the New Jersey Supreme Court ruled 4–3 against Carter's appeal.

The sorry little tale of Mr. Bello shows how complex the Carter trial had become. The whole conviction had rested on Bello's identification of Carter and Artis. Now Bello said he just gave whatever story was asked of him.

Rubin and his new supporters from Canada could only shake their heads in disbelief.

But Rubin knew that his case had long ago ceased to deal with truth. It no longer mattered who was where the night of the shooting. It no longer mattered who saw what and when. All that mattered, in the eyes of the courts, was one thing: Had Rubin Carter been given a fair trial?

To his new Canadian friends, the Rubin Carter case was fresh and interesting. In order to fully understand it, they started examining every bit of information they could. They looked for more. They fed information to the lawyers.

They combed through witness statements, traced car dealers across North America looking for a version of the car Rubin had driven the night of the shooting. In

Kingston, Ontario, and in Northern Ontario they found a Dodge Polara and a Dodge Monaco.

They found the Monaco and Polara shared a similar design of rear lights. However, the Dodge Polara had sculpted lines across the trunk, but had only small tail lights and brake lights on the rear corners. The Monaco, on the other hand, had tail lights and brake lights that lit up across the whole rear of the car. In daylight, they looked similar. At night, only the Monaco "lit up like a butterfly."

To repeat: Carter drove a Polara.

The Canadians traced how each witness had changed testimony over time. All of this they put on a huge spreadsheet, which they mailed to Myron Beldock.

Rubin and Lisa Peters fell in love.

Lesra continued to visit, and to talk to Rubin on the telephone. His schooling continued, and in 1983, he completed high school as an Ontario Scholar — a provincial award given those with an A (above 80 per cent) average. He was on his way to college.

Back in prison, Rubin Carter and his lawyers had to make a decision.

A lawyer, Robert Caruso, who had once worked for the prosecutor's office, had kept a file on parts of the case. The file showed that police and prosecutors had twisted and changed facts to gain a conviction.

This file could be used, they argued, to launch another state appeal. That would drag the case on for many more months, perhaps years. Rubin, anxious to start a new life with Peters, felt he could not wait that long.

Rubin decided to go for what football fans call a "Hail Mary" pass: to throw the ball and hope.

In Rubin's case, they decided to appeal directly to the Supreme Court without further reference to New Jersey.

This meant that they had to prove two things: first, that the trial had been unfair; and second, now that they had gotten this far on process, that Rubin Carter was innocent. It was a slim hope. Only three in one hundred such cases won.

The case was heard before Judge H. Lee Sarokin in February 1985.

It met with delays. The prosecutors dragged their feet.

By now the transcripts and case law had grown in size. To read it all would take years. Perhaps a lifetime.

In November 1985, Judge Sarokin ruled that the lie detector test with Bello should have been shared with defence.

As well, he said that in the second trial (1976), the prosecution had argued that Carter and Artis had committed the murders in revenge for the killing of Eddie Rawls's stepfather. Judge Sarokin insisted that the prosecutors show some proof to back up this "revenge" motive. They could not.

Judge Sarokin's final ruling: Carter's rights had been violated, making the trials unfair.

Rubin Carter was set free, pending appeals.

The state of New Jersey prosecutors did not give up easily. Appeals took another two and a half years.

Finally, the state of New Jersey decided against a third trial. On February 9, 1988, Rubin "Hurricane" Carter was freed of all charges.

It had taken twenty-one years and four months.

By then, Rubin "Hurricane" Carter had spent almost all his life in detention, the U.S. Army, or jail. The unjust conviction had cost him his boxing career, an eye, and his family.

Despite this, he left prison with hope, a belief in humanity, and a burning drive to fight injustice.

He said that prison was the best thing that ever happened to him.

15

CHAPTER FIFTEEN

RESCUING OTHERS

Once free, Rubin Carter left the United States and moved north to Canada.

Trying to enter Canada, Rubin was met by a Canadian guard who questioned his background. Sensitive to racism, Rubin began to bristle. He could feel the old Hurricane arising.

Why was this guy hassling him?

The guard persisted. Had he been to prison? What for?

The answers could have been alarming: Rubin had been convicted of murder — twice.

The guard, now sure of who he was talking to, offered a handshake:

Welcome to Canada.

Hurricane settled into life with the Canadians. The group had spent close to $500,000 in fighting for his freedom. Carter made up his mind to repay it. He helped authors Terry Swinton and Sam Chaiton in the research and promotion of the book *Lazarus and the Hurricane*. This book tells the story of the commune, Lesra, and the freeing of Rubin Carter. He took on speaking engagements to promote the book.

The stuttering, tongue-tied child had become a captivating orator.

More important, he got involved in support of Guy Paul Morin.

Guy Paul Morin was a twenty-five-year-old amateur musician who had been charged with the 1984 murder and rape of Christine Jessop. Jessop, nine years old, lived next door to where Morin lived with his parents in Queensville, Ontario. In the trial, he was found not guilty.

The Crown prosecutors appealed. In a second trial, Morin was found guilty and sentenced to life in prison. Unusual for child sex offenders, he served his term in the general prison population at Kingston Penitentiary.

(For the complete story, read *Real Justice: Guilty of Being Weird, The Story of Guy Paul Morin* by Cynthia J. Faryon.)

With the support of the commune, Rubin became involved. He spoke on behalf of Morin. He worked with the committee that continued to work to free Morin.

When life with Lisa Peters and the other Canadians became strained, Hurricane left. For a time, he moved in with Lesra.

Now he needed money to live on. The Guy Paul Morin committee stepped forward, and gave him a small salary for six months. This kept Rubin involved in the fight for justice for others and gave meaning to his life.

Eventually, DNA testing proved that Guy Paul Morin was innocent. In January 1995, he was acquitted of all charges.

Buoyed by this success, the committee that had taken the Morin case saw other cases of unjust convictions. To keep the team of lawyers and interested citizens together, they created a new organization: The Association in Defence of the Wrongly Convicted (AIDWYC).

An executive director was hired to head the organization. His name was Rubin Carter.

The Hurricane was unleashed to help others in the fight against injustice.

AFTER THE BELL I

FIGHTING FOR OTHERS

With the founding of AIDWYC, Rubin Carter became the focus for unjust convictions in Canada.

In the years since its founding, AIDWYC has been involved in freeing eighteen people in Canada who were unjustly convicted. Many who had tried for years to prove innocence and gain freedom now had a task force to help.

Among the many helped by AIDWYC were Steven Truscott, David Milgaard, Robert Baltovich, Tammy Marquardt, and Romeo Phillion. A full list can be found on the AIDWYC website.

The organization was also involved in seeking compensation for the wrongfully convicted Donald Marshall, Jr.

In the years after leaving the commune, Rubin Carter continued to work for AIDWYC. He gave speeches to any group who would listen: businesses, organizations, and especially to high-school groups. It was on one such visit that he met Ken Klonsky, then a high-school teacher in Toronto, Canada. Rubin and Klonsky got on well. Klonsky, who wrote the Foreword to this book, was involved with Rubin in writing *Eye of the Hurricane: My Path from Darkness to Freedom*.

Throughout his years in prison, Rubin pushed his lawyers relentlessly. Over the years he had differences with (and later became friends with) his first wife, Tee (Mae Thelma). He was also estranged for some time from most of his own brothers and sisters. He fought with Lisa Peters, likely the only woman, he said, who taught him about equality, love, and give and take.

He even became estranged from Lesra over a misunderstanding about a sale of a car.

Even his long association with AIDWYC ended in a misunderstanding. Crown Attorney Susan MacLean had been involved in the Guy Paul Morin case from the beginning. After the first trial freed Morin, she pushed hard for an appeal. She was the lead prosecutor in the second trial that convicted Morin. Even after Morin was finally freed, she uttered bitter comments, which she soon retracted.

In 2005, she was appointed as a judge.

Rubin Carter firmly believed that as executive director of AIDWYC, it was his duty to object to MacLean's appointment. The board of directors of AIDWYC disagreed. Most of the board were close friends who had worked closely with Rubin for twelve years. When the board did not support him, Rubin resigned.

He had been the first leader of AIDWYC and held the position for twelve years, from 1993 to 2005.

AFTER THE BELL II

HURRICANE: THE MOVIE

When they made a movie of his life, Rubin Carter realized he was famous.

He had been a world-class boxer, and had gone a full fifteen rounds with a world champion.

He had written a book that became a best-seller. He became a popular cause. Sports and entertainment figures of the day came to his support. A popular song was written about him.

When he was eventually freed, more books were written about him.

But when the movie came out, he discovered what it really meant to be famous.

Veteran director Norman Jewison directed it: *The Hurricane.*

The 1999 movie starred Denzel Washington, who was nominated for an Academy Award for his role as

Rubin "Hurricane" Carter. The movie was based on two books: *The Sixteenth Round* and *Lazarus and the Hurricane*.

The movie made Rubin Carter a household name once more. It made his name familiar to two generations born since he first fought for a boxing title.

The movie brought together some of the people portrayed in the story. Lesra and his wife were thrilled by the red-carpet treatment received at the Academy Awards. Rubin was star-struck working with Denzel Washington. Not satisfied with leaving the storytelling to the experts, he worked long and hard with Washington and Jewison to get it right.

They did, and Washington's nomination for best actor shows that. But Hollywood is Hollywood, and movies are not documentaries.

The movie told the story of Rubin's battle against racism, and the story of his fight for exoneration. Because it was a Hollywood movie, it served up the emotional highlights of the story: Rubin's tough, angry soul early on, his redemption by love, and his generosity at the end.

It is a version of the greatest story ever told.

AFTER THE BELL III

DR. RUBIN CARTER

In 2011, prior to the release of his last book, *Eye of the Hurricane*, Rubin Carter had been told he had prostate cancer. He was given six months to live.

During the promotion of the book, Rubin began to suffer. Ken Klonsky, who worked with Rubin on the writing and promotion of the book, said Carter never let on. In video recordings of interviews during this time, he maintained his avuncular telling of his inspiring story.

"Prison was the best thing that ever happened to me," Rubin repeated during that book tour. "It made me face myself and made me into the person that I have become."

Though by ghetto standards, his parents were not poor, the ghetto poverty itself grinds away at all who live there. Rubin started as a ghetto-snipe kid. He became an angry, macho boxer, who hurt people for a living.

Prison turned him into a philosopher and humanitarian whose goal was to help other victims of wrongful conviction.

With a Grade 8 education, he ended up with two honorary doctorates and became Dr. Rubin Carter. With good humour, he would remind interviewers that he was no longer "Hurricane."

No, he would chuckle, he was Dr. Rubin Carter now.

AFTER THE BELL IV

THE HEROES

There are many heroes in the story of Dr. Rubin Carter. His lawyer Myron Beldock put in hundreds and hundreds of hours on the case without pay. The Canadian commune provided financial and moral support when it was needed most.

Lesra appeared and became the emotional link to the world that Rubin needed right then. Rescued by the Canadians, Lesra went on to earn several degrees.

Lesra's story shines a light on how books and learning to read are necessary to fulfill dreams. "And you must dream your own dreams," he says. "Not someone else's dream."

Lesra fulfilled his own dream and became a lawyer. For a time he served as a Crown prosecutor. He is now an inspirational speaker.

"Had strangers not come into my life to provide me

with an opportunity, I would not be here today," he told a gathering in London, Ontario. "Those who grew up without that opportunity ended up either on drugs or dead."

But the real hero of the Rubin Carter story is John Artis, the quiet, polite teenager who just wanted to hang out for a while with his hero.

John Artis never wavered. His story never changed. Even when offered deals that would have freed him, he refused to turn against Rubin.

Finally on parole, and finally freed, Artis went on to live his own life.

But when Rubin was diagnosed with cancer, it was John Artis who arrived at his side. As the horrid disease consumed Rubin's powerful body and wracked him with pain, John Artis was his caregiver.

Rubin "Hurricane" Carter died on April 17, 2014.

One person was at his side: John Artis.

No one had a truer friend.

AUTHOR'S NOTE

In researching this complex story of a complex man, I have as much as possible consulted original documents. In many cases, this was impossible. Strangely enough, the richest source of documents came from an odd source. Cal Deal, a former reporter, has spent many years trying to convince the world that Rubin Carter was guilty. He's wrong, of course. He makes the same mistakes the police made originally, jumping from a possibility to probability with no logical steps. However, his website The Graphic Witness does provide links to some original police documents, although he is very selective about what documents he presents.

My one regret is that I never did get to meet Rubin Carter. Part of this was by design: In my research, I wanted to digest as much as possible about the case before I talked to anyone. Alas, when I arrived at the point of feeling that I could talk somewhat intelligently about the case, it was too late. Rubin Carter died, literally, the week I was finishing the manuscript.

My special thanks to Ken Klonsky, who generously agreed to writing the Foreword to this fascinating story. Ken worked with Hurricane on *Eye of the Hurricane* both in writing and promotion of that book.

My personal salute to Rubin Carter and to John

Artis. It is impossible to imagine how such a devastating injustice challenges the human spirit. Rubin showed the spirit of a true champion, refusing to be sucked into anger and despair. John Artis stuck by his friend and hero even when betraying him undoubtedly would have gained him freedom.

This version of the Hurricane Carter story relies on the accounts from several sources (listed below in the Bibliography). Where versions of events vary, I have examined the evidence and have done my best to present the most likely narrative. Any errors that have crept in are solely my creations.

Rubin, Rest In Peace.

GLOSSARY

ACQUITTAL: the verdict when someone accused of a crime is found not guilty.

APPEAL: a request to review a case that has already been decided in court. An appeal must be based on points of law or, in rare cases, a change in evidence or testimony. In the United States, an appeal must first be presented to the State Supreme Court before it can be heard by the federal Supreme Court.

ASSAILANT: a person accused of beating up or attacking another person.

BOOTLEGGER: someone who sells liquor illegally.

CONVICTION: the verdict when someone accused of a crime is found guilty.

COUNSEL: lawyer.

CROSS-EXAMINATION: After a witness for either the defence or for the Crown tells what he or she knows, a lawyer for the other side gets to ask questions of the witness.

CROWN ATTORNEY: the lawyer(s) acting for the government, or "the Crown," in court proceedings. They are the prosecutors in Canada's legal system. Sometimes called Crown Counsel.

DEFENDANT: the person who has been formally accused of and charged with committing a crime.

DIALYSIS: a medical procedure to clear urine from the blood when kidneys have failed.

EXONERATED: found to be free of blame.

FABRICATION: made up; lies.

FULL DISCLOSURE: revealing important or requested evidence to the other side in a trial. In 1991 (largely due to the Donald Marshall Jr. case) the Supreme Court of Canada ruled that the Crown had a duty to reveal its evidence to the defence before a trial. Before 1991, disclosure was voluntary.

INDICTMENT: a formal charge against an individual.

JURY: A criminal trial is decided by a group of twelve randomly-selected citizens from the province in which the trial is held. All twelve must agree on a verdict.

MINORITY: a small part of a whole. In society, persons of a race who are not the same as most others. If those persons have racial features they are often referred to as visible minorities.

PAROLE: release from prison before the full sentence has been served. A prisoner on parole must agree to certain restrictions and report regularly to a parole officer.

PEERS: people of a similar legal status.

PENITENTIARY: a prison for serving sentences of more than two years. Maximum security prisons operate under heavy security. Minimum security prisons allow more freedom for prisoners.

PERJURY: lying in a court of law. It is a crime.

PERPETRATOR: someone guilty of an act.

PRELIMINARY HEARING: a hearing held to decide if there is enough evidence for a trial. This is held after the accused has been charged with a crime.

PROBATION: a sentence imposed often on young offenders in place of prison or jail.

PROSECUTOR: a lawyer acting for the State. In Canada this is referred to as Crown Attorney; in the U.S. as Prosecuting Attorney..

RACIALIZED: having to do with the race of people involved. Donald Marshall, Jr. was treated badly in part because of his race.

RACISM: having to do with race, usually in a negative way.

RULING: a decision made by a judge during a court hearing.

(SIC): so it is in the original. In a quoted passage, this indicates a word is used as it appears in the source.

TESTIMONY: the statement of a witness under oath.

TRANSCRIPTS: word-for-word written reports of a trial.

VERDICT: the decision of the jury at the end of a trial, usually guilty or not guilty.

ADDITIONAL RESOURCES

For those looking for more information on the fascinating story of Rubin Carter, the following books, movies, online videos, and websites are suggested.

BOOKS:
Eye of the Hurricane: My Path from Darkness to Freedom by Dr. Rubin "Hurricane" Carter, LL.D. with Ken Klonsky. Published 2011 by Lawrence Hill Books, Chicago, Illinois. ISBN 978-1-56976-568-5.

Hurricane: The Miraculous Journey of Rubin Carter by James S. Hirsch. Published 2000 by Mariner Books / Houghton Mifflin Company, New York, New York. ISBN 978-0-618-08728-0.

Lazarus and the Hurricane: The Untold Story of the Freeing of Rubin "Hurricane" Carter by Sam Chaiton and Terry Swinton. Published 1991 by Viking, Toronto, Ontario. ISBN 0-670-83482-3.

Rubin Hurricane Carter and the American Justice System by Paul B. Wice. Published 2000 by Rutgers University Press, New Brunswick, New Jersey. ISBN 0-8135-2864-X

The Sixteenth Round: From Number 1 Contender to Number 45472, by Rubin "Hurricane" Carter. Published 2011 by Lawrence Hill Books, Chicago, Illinois. ISBN 978-1-56976-567-8.

MOVIES:

The Hurricane (1999) directed by Norman Jewison, starring Denzel Washington, written by Kenneth Chisholm (from the books *The Sixteenth Round* by Rubin Carter and *Lazarus and the Hurricane* by Sam Chaiton and Terry Swinton), released January 2000 by Universal Studios Entertainment, a division of NBC Universal.

HURRICANE CARTER'S FIGHTS:

A number of Hurricane Carter's boxing matches are available online through YouTube and other sources. I provide a selection of such links below. There are many more.

Carter–Ellis:
www.youtube.com/watch?v=jgwBfzbBr0k

Carter–Fernadez:
www.youtube.com/watch?v=k0LQ5EXSNXI

Carter–Giardello:
www.youtube.com/watch?v=8nJMLyUz_Qo

Carter–Gomeo Brennan:
www.youtube.com/watch?v=0BrGa5YBqp0

Carter–Griffith:
www.youtube.com/watch?v=kgDxA78CJho

Carter–Mims:
www.youtube.com/watch?v=K67SnkC11IU

INTERVIEWS WITH RUBIN CARTER:
Interview with Rubin "Hurricane" Carter by Sting-
ray Body Art and Metropolitan Pictures President
Scott Matalon and Boston Boxing & Fitness owner Ed
Lavache on Sept 11, 2010:
www.youtube.com/watch?v=nJETGOnQi8s

Dr. Rubin 'Hurricane' Carter as keynote speaker (from
Speakers Spotlight):
www.youtube.com/watch?v=nhKew1z2UcY

KSTP-TV host Sheletta Brundidge interviews Rubin 'Hurricane' Carter:
www.youtube.com/watch?v=VOs9pP-m43g

WEBSITES:
The Association in Defence of the Wrongly Convicted:
www.aidwyc.org

Ken Klonsky's site Outing the Law: A Website on Injustice: www.kenklonsky.com

Lesra Martin as a motivational speaker: www.lesra.com

INDEX